# A SMALL DOOR SET IN CONCRETE

# A SMALL DOOR SET IN CONCRETE

*One Woman's Story of Challenging Borders in Israel/Palestine*

**ILANA HAMMERMAN**

Translated by Tal Haran

*The University of Chicago Press* ✳ *Chicago and London*

The University of Chicago Press, Chicago 60637
The University of Chicago Press, Ltd., London
© 2019 by Ilana Hammerman
Published 2019
Printed in the United States of America

28  27  26  25  24  23  22  21  20  19      1  2  3  4  5

ISBN-13: 978-0-226-66631-0 (cloth)
ISBN-13: 978-0-226-66645-7 (e-book)
DOI: https://doi.org/10.7208/chicago/9780226666457.001.0001

Originally published in Hebrew as *Isha Levada* © Achuzat Bayit 2016
Published by arrangement with
The Institute for the Translation of Hebrew Literature

Library of Congress Cataloging-in-Publication Data

Names: Hammerman, Ilana, author. | Haran, Tal, translator.
Title: A small door set in concrete : one woman's story of challenging
borders in Israel/Palestine / Ilana Hammerman ; translated by Tal Haran.
Description: Chicago: University of Chicago Press, 2019.
Identifiers: LCCN 2019024409 | ISBN 9780226666310 (cloth) |
ISBN 9780226666457 (ebook)
Subjects: LCSH: Arab-Israeli conflict—Psychological aspects. |
Jewish-Arab relations.
Classification: LCC DS128.2 .H365 2019 | DDC 956.04—dc23
LC record available at https://lccn.loc.gov/2019024409

♾ This paper meets the requirements of ANSI/NISO Z39.48–1992
(Permanence of Paper).

*To Daniella Carmi, friend and writer*
*whose voice is unique in Israeli literature*

Even through walls bloweth my free breath,
and into prisons and imprisoned spirits!

FRIEDRICH NIETZSCHE, *Thus Spake Zarathustra*

# CONTENTS

# FOREWORD

## David Shulman

There are people who are formed in such a way that they simply cannot bear the sight, or even the knowledge, of injustice and suffering inflicted upon others. Some, probably most, of them simply turn away with varying degrees of shame, probably hidden from awareness. Others are impelled to act. Why some people who feel moral outrage are driven to act while others are not is one of the mysteries. Each activist—I have known many—has her or his own story. Motivations are always complex and compounded; they are also largely irrelevant to the action itself. In nearly all who do this work there is a nontrivial strand of imaginative empathy, whatever else comes into play.

I first came to know Ilana Hammerman during the demonstrations in the Sheikh Jarrah neighborhood of Jerusalem, from 2009 to 2011, when the municipality and the government were intent on expelling Palestinians from homes they had been living in for over half a century. The Israeli civil courts went along with these plans. Then, as now, Ilana advocated mass civil disobedience as the preferred, and possibly the only really effective, mode of resistance to the abhorrent policies of the

right. Peaceful activists in Sheikh Jarrah were routinely arrested,
often with extreme violence, by police and soldiers in the course
of the demonstrations—which, partly because of this violence,
won international visibility and were thus eventually successful
in deterring the authorities from further expulsions. That was a
little less than ten years ago; sad to say, the threat of large-scale
dispossession of Palestinian families living in Sheikh Jarrah has
recently been renewed. One might ask: are there, today, enough
Israelis ready and able to adopt nonviolent civil disobedience
as a consistent tactic in protest against the occupation and its
evils? Are there enough to make a difference? Gone are the days
when four hundred thousand ordinary Israeli citizens came out
to demonstrate against Ariel Sharon's role as defense minister
when several thousand Palestinians in the Lebanese refugee
camps of Sabra and Shatila were massacred by the Christian
Phalangists. These events took place in the autumn of 1982. I'm
not sure we could now muster much more than a minyan of
ten righteous men and women, not counting the few hundred
Israeli activists still on their feet.

But moral outrage that seeks action doesn't make such calculations. Nor should it. I can tell you from my own experience
that the crimes one sees in the Occupied Territories, literally every hour, are enough to infuriate anyone endowed with a conscience. They can drive one mad. And there is still a semblance
of power in the public voice of outrage. Some years ago there
was a workshop at the Van Leer Institute in Jerusalem on peace
and Palestine and the occupation. There were presentations by
well-known figures on the left followed by the usual ineffectual
discussions. But at some point Ilana spoke from the audience,
with clarity and courage, of the urgent need for all of us to
break the law—that is, the cruel and indeed illegal laws of the

occupation—and she outlined ways we could do it. We could, for example, follow her in driving Palestinians from the West Bank across the Green Line into Israel for a day on the beach, or to reach a hospital, or to visit family or friends. We could lie down in the face of the bulldozers the army regularly sends to demolish Palestinian houses. We could stop paying taxes. And so on. Sari Nusseibeh, then the president of Al-Quds University, was with us that day, and he was amazed and moved by this turn in the discussion; he said he wished his colleagues at Al-Quds were there to hear it, since they might not believe that Israelis were capable of even thinking such thoughts.

Ilana has a gift. She cuts through the sluggishness and passivity that nearly all of us have when confronted with Israel's policies toward Palestinian people and Palestinian land. I asked her how she acquired this gift. She said it began with curiosity about the society that lives right next door but that Israelis hardly know. "I'm an adventurer," she said. "That is part of my freedom." She means crossing the border into Palestinian villages and homes, heedless of risks and rules. The book you are about to read tells the story of those adventures. It is an honest, beautifully written account of a daring woman, often alone in the wilder places of the West Bank and Gaza, going wherever her human values and her instincts take her. As always, the journey is also one of introspection and intimate discovery, which she spells out.

The beginning was also bound up with language, the key that opens hearts and doors. She began learning Arabic in order to communicate with Arab workers in her home. (It is astonishing to me that so few Israelis take this simple step.) Then she studied Arabic at the Hebrew University, and she learned, as one does, by speaking with people. She says that knowing

Arabic changed everything, and she's right about that. She has
lived with many Palestinian women (and here and there saved
a life); her voice is that of a woman among women who may
not be able to make their voices heard. As she said to me about
her childhood in Haifa, "I was taught from the start not to be
silent."

Her first arrest came in 1991, and it changed her life—much
for the better. A relatively large group of Israelis, predominantly
women, were protesting house demolitions by the army in
Qalqiliya, on the West Bank. They were arrested and held in
jail for five days. In those not-so-distant days, the minds of the
police had not yet been entirely poisoned by the hysterical na-
tionalism that is raging through the public spaces today. Those
arrested were treated well; they even celebrated a birthday, with
their captors, on their way to jail. The case never went to trial,
but those five days were memorable—also fun. Ilana lost her
fear. I know something of what she felt. Today, inexplicably, as I
have seen with my own eyes, the police and the soldiers usually
fail to fulfill her earnest wish to be sent to jail again.

She could have named her book "A Woman in Dark Times,"
as a gesture to Hannah Arendt's *Men in Dark Times* (where
were the women then?). A very unusual woman at that. That's
the thing about dark times: in the midst of the silent masses,
every once in a while one meets some courageous human being
using her imagination and her grit to do the decent thing, to
cross the borders and the concrete walls and the barbed wire,
both material and mental, and to befriend the innocent and the
oppressed on the other side. Ilana is not the only such person
in today's Israel, but few have the eloquence, the passionate
assurance, and the irony she brings to her stories. They make
for compelling reading, and they are often, despite everything,

illumined by flashes of lighthearted insouciance. They are also highly relevant to bitter struggles far from the tiny strip of land between the Jordan and the sea. Henry David Thoreau, in whose footsteps we follow, was no doubt referring to Ilana when he wrote, "All good things are wild and free."

# PROLOGUE

# In the Land of the Maoris

"On your own? A woman on her own doesn't travel like this around here," she was told by the innkeeper in East Cape, New Zealand, where she began a solo bike trip. "A woman on her own would never ride a bicycle here along these empty roads. You'll be robbed. Might even be raped. The indigenous live out here, you know. This is Maori country. They can be violent, the Maoris. You can't possibly understand each other. Forget this trip of yours. Give up and go back!"

"You're on your own? A woman on her own? Aren't you afraid? A woman could never hike these trails on her own!" said a couple she encountered on her second day of hiking. She had been relieved to see a pair of hikers in this hilly landscape where she had until then only passed animals grazing and had grown frustrated with the unclear markings on her map. She asked them if she was on the right path. "Yes, this is the right way, but don't hike here on your own. A woman on her own doesn't do so. Go back!" They scowled at her and proceeded in the opposite direction.

This was only the beginning of her trip in East Cape.

What is the right path, from where to where? Over and over she had asked herself this question at the turn of the third millennium. which had got off to a very bad start in her personal life. She asked and answered: the right way for her now was to the ends of the earth. The right way for her now was away from death, which had snatched from her, in one single year—no, eleven months, no, all of eternity—both her life partner and her only sister. The right way for her now was turning from the deaths of these two people, from their final and absolute disappearance, to the ends of the earth.

Perhaps one could abandon this world at the ends of the earth?

She had spread out a world map on the floor of her Jerusalem apartment, her eyes wandering over it as her fingers roamed and chose New Zealand. In New Zealand she had opted for the northeastern tip of North Island, East Cape, and in East Cape a certain small town, to serve as the point of departure for her bicycle journey.

And so she set off.

Having flown over twenty hours in three different planes, she landed at a third airport, from which she drove to the city of Auckland. After staying there for a few days, she rode a rented bicycle to the bus station and bought a bus ticket to that small town she had pinpointed. She stuck the bicycle in the tall, narrow luggage compartment at the back of the bus, pushed and pushed until it stood on its handles somehow, pressed in between suitcases and bags in an unnatural, ungainly way, and went to take a seat at the front of the bus. She rode and rode and rode. Nine hours passed before she finally arrived at that small town and entered a little inn, requesting a room where she could spend the night. The innkeeper asked her where she was headed and whether she was on her own. When she answered, the innkeeper exclaimed, "A woman on her own? No, impossible! A woman on her own doesn't take bicycle trips out here, in wild Maori country. Don't even try it. Go back to Auckland!"

But there was no way she would give up and turn back. Arising early the next morning, she walked over to the bicycle in the yard, expecting to load her red backpack on it and get going. But she couldn't manage. It was impossible to tie the heavy, bulky pack to the bike, as its pockets were bursting with items. Each time she tried to secure it, it would tip and drop to a different side of the bike. And so in a fit of anger she threw it down, leaned over it, undid its ties and buckles, and unloaded about a quarter of its contents into the nearby dumpster. Then she refastened its buckles, pulled its cords tight, and lifted it. Though it was not really much thinner now, she began again to secure it to the bicycle frame, pulling and winding and stretching elastic straps around the pack, looking for places to hook them on to the metal frame, the saddle post, and the rear fork, spots that were not meant for this at all. But the hooks released, nicking her hands, further infuriating her. She kept at it, pinching them between thumb and index finger, pulling them over to other hooking points and forcing them to fit until the pack was smothered in its shackles, crooked and humpbacked but bound tight. And so she mounted the seat. One of the backpack's pockets pressed uncomfortably against her buttocks, but shoving it brought no relief. Finally she set off.

Then she realized immediately that the front tire had been punctured.

She got off the saddle again, bent over, unscrewed the hub, pulled the wheel toward her, and sat down, straining her back in the process, to remove the faulty tire. With a yellow plastic spoon she had brought for this purpose, she yanked the tire's stiff edges out of its groove. She pulled out the flawed tubing and threw it aside. She took a new tube out of its wrap and blew into it, then carefully and smoothly secured it inside the tire; with even greater effort, she replaced the tire in its groove inside the wheel, taking care not to let the thin tube bunch up inside the thick tire. She then fitted the whole wheel with its hub into place in the front of the bicycle and screwed it back on. She unclipped a small pump from the bicycle frame, placed it, and blew, inflating the tire as best she could. At last she straddled the seat once more and began pedaling.

She estimated it would be a ten-day north-south bicycle ride along the ocean shore, including some hikes. Back at Auckland's tourist information bureau, she had sketched out the route along a detailed roadmap of East Cape. And now, after so much effort and such a long journey, on her very first hiking trail, a couple tells her that a woman on her own should not, must not, hike the trails here in wild Maori country. "For they will rob you, rape you, maybe even murder you."


"A woman on her own?" the first Maori woman she had ever met asked her as they stood along a riverbank in the land of the Maoris. This Maori woman had been accompanied by a Maori man, no longer young but still strong of build, dressed in light-colored jeans and a dark blue windbreaker. Perhaps because his eyes, probably a bit elongated like hers, were hidden behind large sunglasses, his only distinctive feature was just one front tooth that showed in his mouth, a single tooth in a large grin on a pleasant oval face, not light-complexioned but not very dark either.

The Maori couple had a small motorboat in which they

took travelers across the river to the rain forests—a sign to that effect, advertising a one-hour boat ride for a reasonable fee, had led her to swerve off the road. Back in East Cape the innkeeper had told her that the tourist season had not yet begun and she would therefore be quite alone on the road, and indeed she was the only passenger to climb into the man's boat to ride down the river. The Maori woman, likely this boatman's wife, remained on shore with her bicycle and backpack.

The man drove her for a whole hour in the small motorboat. She perched on the back bench and he guided from the front, a yellow-and-white life jacket over his windbreaker and a matching life buoy about his neck. The channel grew narrower as the boat moved downriver, passing through thickly rounded swaths of giant ferns, and behind them bushes and tall trees, that pressed closer and closer to the boat until they seemed to be closing in on the boatman and rider. Occasionally the man would turn off the engine and let the boat drift, just kissing the riverbank, giving the woman traveler time to gaze in silence into all this wild abundance. In silence, for he never spoke, he didn't even smile anymore, and sometimes he would point somewhere, perhaps at a particular plant or bird, and the woman who was with him would squint to follow his finger, but she could discern only a dark, enormous tangle of mazes and mysteries. After about half an hour the man turned the boat back, and another half hour later, the boatman and his passenger had returned to the point of departure. The Maori woman met their arrival and helped the man pull the boat in to its mooring. She reached out to the passenger and helped her step out of the lightly rocking boat and climb to the shore.

Once the passenger regained her land legs, she hurried to make sure her bike and backpack were still where she had left them. Indeed they were, the pack shackled to the bike frame in a clumsy confusion of colored elastic straps. The white woman paid the Maori woman for the boat ride. It was then that the Maori woman asked her, "A woman on her own, eh?" and proceeded to warn her, "No good. Not good at all. You should be careful, be mindful. Perhaps you should at least know how to say hello in Maori, so as to seem friendly." She began to repeat the Maori word for "hello," and the white woman watched the movement her lips made, then repeated the sounds.

"You might want to smile a little," the Maori woman hinted with a toothy grin. The white woman tried to stretch her lips into a smile as she said goodbye. Slightly embarrassed, she hurried over to her bike and rode away.

But during the next few days in East Cape she encountered no one to say hello to in Maori. On one side of the empty road she took, there were soft green rolling hills strewn with white sheep as far as the eye could see, and on the other side, steep slopes overgrown with green ferns that dropped toward the blue sea.

Once not far from her a herd of bulls crossed the road and she grew frightened: they could be violent, they could attack, gore her with their horns, kick, kill her. She stopped but didn't get off the bicycle—instead she planted her feet on the asphalt on either side and watched the bulls slowly cross the road, dark and enormous. Then she noticed a pickup truck parked by the side of the road, very close to her. A man got out, and another looked out the driver's window. They were not Maori—they were whites—but no matter. Maybe *they* would be violent; maybe they would attack, rape, or murder her. But the man who had emerged from the truck stretched out one arm, apparently marking the way for the passing bulls, setting a barrier between her and them until the last bull crossed. Then the man turned toward her and signaled for her to continue.

And she did, in safety, on her own. No man nor animal harmed her, nor did anyone help her. A woman on her own, riding a bicycle along these empty roads, hiking the winding paths and trails, carefully descending the slopes to the shore among giant ferns, on foot alongside the bicycle, gripping its handles and pulling its brakes, and stretching out on the banks of tiny bays, on her own, widowed, withdrawn, free.

# In the Land of the
# Palestinians

*What on Earth Are You Looking For There?*

In the meantime the third millennium has turned five, ten, fifteen years old, and in those years the woman has been traveling no longer to the ends of the earth but rather not far from her hometown Jerusalem, in the region unofficially known as "the West Bank." Like other smaller sectors within that territory, it had and still has many appellations, depending on the time and speaker: the Occupied Territories, the Held Territories, Judea and Samaria, just plain The Territories, the Palestinian Authority, Area A, Area B, Area C, the Etzyon Bloc, the Binyamin District. Some names link and others separate, but under any name no one—no local or foreigner—can distinguish the exact borders of the whole or its parts, be they geographical, administrative, or political.

There, too, this woman travels mostly on her own, in her car. For a while she had used the old boxy red Ford Fiesta she had purchased with her partner, but she eventually bought a new car on her own. In his memory she chose another red Ford

Fiesta, though she was disappointed that the newer model had a sort of unnecessary aerodynamic design, more curved and elongated. Now, though, this car too is getting old.

Not long ago, when the third millennium was already fifteen, she set off on her own for the West Bank through the Israeli village of Bar Giora, heading for the Palestinian village of Hussan. It was Saturday, a day on which the Jewish state halts all public transportation, and as she passed Tzur Hadassah (another Israeli community) she spotted a young woman raising a hitchhiking thumb. She stopped and picked her up. The young hitchhiker wished to get to Jerusalem, and the woman driver told her she was going to Hussan and could take her on that far. The young hitchhiker hesitated a bit but agreed so she could at least advance toward her destination. She gave the driver a wondering look and asked: "Hussan? It's an Arab village, isn't it?"

"Yes, an Arab village," the driver answered.

"What on earth are you looking for there?" she asked.

"Friends—I've got good friends there," the driver answered.

The young woman shrugged and lapsed into silence. A few kilometers further, she released her safety belt and asked to get out. The older woman stopped at the side of the road. The hitchhiker opened the door and got out, thanked her politely, and closed the door, leaving the lingering scent of a sweet shampoo inside the car.

"What on earth are you looking for there?" Israeli people have been asking her all these years. What business have you in Hussan and Batir and Nahalin and Beit Umar and Sa'ir and Umm Al Kheir and Ramallah and Gaza? She has been young and now she is old, soon she will be ancient, yet Israelis never stop asking her that question, dozens, hundreds of times. What on earth could you want in "the Territories," in Arab places? *Lots!* she answers, usually to herself. She has plenty to seek out in "the Territories," in Arab places. And she finds plenty there too: different landscapes and life, culture and customs. She finds and learns a new language, different from her own yet still very close. She meets people, spends hours or sometimes days and nights in their midst. She is taken into the bosoms of large families that keep growing—she, whose own family was progressively reduced by disasters, has become familiar with women and men and children in their hours of joy and grief, with their strengths and vulnerabilities; she has shared with them her own joy and grief, her own strengths and vulnerabilities.

Owing to the political circumstances into which she was born, in these local trips she finds something more precious than her discoveries in far-flung places. She finds something she has learned is more important to her than anything else: freedom. And not just any freedom but a certain kind of freedom: the freedom of crossing with her body and spirit and mind barriers of walls and fences, ignoring borders of stone and metal and laws and decrees, and challenging the borders of the soul: borders of subjugation and obedience, and especially of fear. And defeating them.

And along with this freedom she has also discovered a new kind of joie de vivre.

## *A Flat Tire*

Two women in abayas (long dresses) and hijabs (headkerchiefs) waved to her from the side of the potholed road. This time she

was neither riding her bicycle nor walking along hilly trails; she
was driving her red Ford Fiesta along a village street. A woman
on her own, driving a car. This was early on during her trips in
the West Bank.

*You will be kidnapped, sequestered, captured, murdered.* Why
were they waving at her? She slowed down, took a good look
at them, one young, the other an older woman. She hit the
brakes and pressed the button to let the window down. After
the window went all the way down, she got scared and pressed
the button to raise it. And so it went all the way up. She pressed
and lowered it, pressed and raised it, trying to manipulate the
tricky button until the window was only about one-quarter of
the way open, about three-quarters closed.

"Marhaba" (hello), she said. Here she knows how to say
hello. There are no Maoris here; there are Arabs. Arab women.
She is no longer at the ends of the earth and no longer has the
urge to jump off it, not now anyway. She has reached this Arab
village in the West Bank—Hussan.

"Marhabtein" (hello to you too), the women answered, and
pointed down, toward the tires of her car.

She let the window down further, and then some more, but
didn't see a thing. What should she do? She had to lower the
window all the way and stick her head out, there was no other
way. Now she saw it: the back tire, crushed and flattened. Impossible to drive on.

What should she do? Get out of the car? *You will be kidnapped, captured, sequestered, murdered.*

They smiled, the two women.

No choice. She had to get out. And so she did and stood
with them beside her flat-tired car, in the street on the outskirts
of the village.

But the three of them weren't there long on their own. Within just a moment or two they were surrounded by women, men, boys, and children who laughed, asked questions, in Hebrew, in Arabic, chattering without waiting for a reply. One fellow approached her and held out his hand to take the keys she was holding. Before she could decide whether to hang on to them or let them go, the keys were already in his hand.

Another moment or two and the trunk was open, the spare tire out on the ground, and the jack inserted in its proper spot on the underside of the car. The car was lifted, and the flat tire was yanked out and rolled at the feet of cheering children. Two sturdy hands rolled the spare tire as another pair of hands slapped it a bit. Ever so quickly the new tire filled the space left by the old one, now deposited in its compartment in the trunk, and the back end of the car was lowered and the car now stood more assured and decent on the road, and the jack was placed back in its hidden spot under the trunk padding, and the trunk door was slammed shut and the keys back in her hand and she just stood there, confused, slightly defeated, trapped amid this colorful crowd that wished to know who she was and what she was doing there and where and to whom she was headed and what for.

Then suddenly her cell phone buzzed, and a psychiatrist whom she had frantically tried to reach all morning, having just received yet another piece of bad news about family, told her that she was now free to talk. "But *I'm* not free right now," she whispered into the small gadget. "Maybe later, a bit later?" she pleaded. "I need you, I'm in distress, something horrible has happened, I don't know what to do, to tell or not, when, how . . . it's cancer again . . ." All those eyes encircling her, staring and wondering, smiling, ridiculing a bit perhaps, embarrassed her even more until a woman handed her a small cup of sweet black coffee. She gulped it down quickly and felt a little stronger. Thanking them, she hurried to the car and sat down behind the wheel. Starting the engine, she spotted the one-hundred-shekel note that she had offered one of the young men as payment for the repair. Here it was on the seat beside her—payment was not accepted.

A quarter of an hour later she was sitting grief-stricken in the living room of the family she had planned to visit, as she had done every Friday for the past few months, sitting and sobbing within view of Amal, the compassionate mother of the family who had already become a close friend—they had already shared a lot with each other, each from her own existential loneliness. Yasmine, the youngest daughter, with dark, girlish features, was also with them in the living room, staring at their weeping guest with her big brown eyes. The older guest wept unabashedly, taking each tissue that the mother and daughter pulled alertly out of an embroidery-covered box. Their somber guest tried to tell them in her broken Arabic that she and her family members would not be killed by Arabs, it seemed, but by cancer.

## *Passengers*

Always when she passes there in her red Ford Fiesta in the late afternoon, they are standing by the roadside. It is a side road turning right from the main road that leads up to the urban settler colony of Beitar Ilit, and this side road leads to the Palestinian villages of Batir and Hussan and Nahalin, although no

road sign shows that. She is headed to those villages. They—
five, ten, twenty men—stand not far from the turn, beyond
the two large red signs high on metal posts on both the right
and left sides of the road, warning her, to no avail, not to enter:

> This Road Leads To Area "A"
> Under The Palestinian Authority
> Entrance For Israeli
> Citizens Is Forbidden,
> Dangerous To Your Lives
> And Is Against The Israeli Law

At first she hurried past the signs and the men standing beyond them, but lately she has been slowing down and reading
the signs carefully, and several times she took photos of them
through her car window and drove on. Then she began to slow
down when passing the men themselves, and realized they were
mostly quite elderly and wore dusty, stained clothes, probably
workers on their way home. Bags and parcels lay at the feet of
some of the men, and others held only a small plastic bag. They
must have been waiting for some transport to their village—
perhaps a taxi, a neighbor, an acquaintance.

So she began to slow down each time, turn her head in their
direction, try to make eye contact, but they did not notice her;
none of them hailed her for a ride. She realized that she wanted
to stop and take one of them with her, not so much as a favor
as out of some vague whim that had sprouted and bloomed in
her heart, perhaps to prove to herself that she was not afraid,
and perhaps to forge another connection of acquaintance and
closeness with the inhabitants of this strange piece of land she
had now been visiting regularly for months. And perhaps she

was tired of being alone in her car—a whole car just for herself, driving alone and even lonely inside this motorized tin and plastic box, with sounds from outside dulled by the tightly shut windows—while they stood in pairs and groups, a small human hubbub, chatting, smoking cigarettes as if they didn't actually have it so bad, perhaps they were even better off than she was as disasters were latching on to her now, one after another.

But even when she slowed down markedly, they didn't wave to ask for a ride,though she knew very well that most of them had begun their day in the dark of night, perhaps at three or four in the morning.

Just the thought of it gave her a headache; her eyes smarted as they did on days following the nights when sleep had eluded her from three or four in the morning. But she had nothing to get up for at such an hour; she was not required to take a taxi to the Bethlehem checkpoint and stand there in a suffocating and rib-crushing line of people, long, crowded, and nervous between tall barbed-wire fences, or climb up hills and down valleys before dawn in order to bypass the Beitar checkpoint in order to get to a workplace by seven.

There they stood not far from the two large red signs, standing and waiting for a taxi or a neighbor or an acquaintance who might chance by, and she, neither their neighbor nor their acquaintance, would crawl past them, and tell herself that in a matter of moments she could take four of them to their homes easily, charging nothing. But they didn't ask and she didn't offer, but rather stepped on the accelerator and continued along the potholed road that had already cost her one flat tire and several hubcaps that had broken loose and rolled off and left the wheels and grooves in their black nakedness, which she had decided looked better anyway than the superfluous stylish hubcaps that had become the fashion.

Every time she passed the men now she would sense a tinge of excitement, a thrill mixed with a certain dread and unease and curiosity, as well as a desire for human contact and a release from inhibition and fear. Release from the recoil that would initially arise with closeness to one of those men, the fellow in the red-and-white *keffiyeh* (scarf), for instance, who would sit crusty and dusty and sweating on the seat next to her with his unfamiliar scents and speech, and perhaps make her listen to his troubles, which were familiar, and even ask for help that she could not or would not wish to offer: all this accompanied that excited tinge she felt in her chest.

Until one day, when the sight of an old woman among the men made something stream out of her trapped heart straight to the foot on the gas pedal, and the foot rose and hit the brake, hard.

Her red Ford Fiesta stopped and stood. And they finally looked at her. And she shouted her question in Arabic to the woman, only to her:

"Want a lift to Hussan?"

"No, to Batir," several voices answered her from the men's group. No one apparently wanted a lift to Hussan, not even the woman, who didn't answer at all.

Then she remembered that this time she really was going to Batir, first to Batir and only then to Hussan.

"I'm driving to Batir," she called out to the woman.

The woman still ignored her.

"Come on, I'll take you to Batir, I'm going to Batir!" She wouldn't relent.

Some men approached the car.

No, it wasn't them she wanted to take along, she tried to indicate to them—no offense intended—just the woman. There wasn't room enough for all of them anyway: the excuse suddenly hit her and she turned to indicate the backseat covered by the gray sheet that belonged to Momo the dog, replete with light brown hairs.

But the car doors had already swung open front and back, and the old woman, who had come closer in the meantime, entered and landed heavily on the front seat (she was actually heavy, and perhaps not so old as the driver had thought), while two men climbed into the back, and a third man collected all the parcels from the ground, and the woman's bag, as if they had coordinated it all between them to perfection, and went to the trunk and opened it, and the driver watched him in the rear-view mirror, lifting and shoving in a large cardboard box tied with string, two full-to-bursting black plastic bags, and a cloth-covered wicker basket, then closing the trunk and squeezing into the backseat with determination and skill and speed in spite of the two other men's big bodies.

The red Ford Fiesta got on its way somewhat unwillingly, coughing a little, refusing to surrender to fourth gear, slowing down to third gear uphill, groaning and snorting into second gear. But inside, what life suddenly blossomed in that inner space, shouts and laughter and stories. Her four passengers never fell silent for a moment. She didn't know whether they were gossiping or joking—she understood very little of their rural speech patterns—but she sensed life and was glad of it.

At some point they remembered that she was there and asked her who she was and where she was going.

To Bassem's, she answered; she was on her way to see Bassem and his family, he was a good friend of hers, Bassem, she exaggerated, almost bragged. And knew she was trying to regain some confidence.

Bassem? Which Bassem? they asked her.

Bassem . . . Bassem . . . Bassem Abu . . . Abu . . . what was his son's name? And the father's, the family's?

Really, what *was* the family name? No, she didn't know the name of his family. How awkward—after all, she does know Bassem pretty well. They weren't exactly brother and sister, but he had already been to her home, had come to help her find the hiding place of the family of mice that had nested there not long ago. And he found it! Incredible how many hiding places for mice he'd discovered in her apartment in a very short time. Incredible how he knew what to take apart and move around for the purpose.

But she couldn't tell them his family name, and all the Bassems with their sons and fathers and grandfathers whom the men suggested to her didn't help—there were many Bassems in Batir, it seemed.

"Wait till we get there and you'll see," she told them, and made them laugh. She is perhaps a bit of a wit, she thought, and not for the first time. Sometimes she really thought she was a bit funny, a woman who pondered and wondered a lot, and never very quick at adapting, especially when roaming in foreign parts, which she had done a lot in recent years years—in the land of the Maoris, for example, and also among women sold into prostitution, from Kishinev to Tel Aviv and Haifa.

And now here, among these villages.

She no longer minded that she might seem funny to them: they had been laughing earlier too, and who cares? The world is funny, so one laughs. She felt at ease, her embarrassment was gone, gone were her fears, the dread—*you'll be kidnapped! mur-*

*dered! a woman on her own!* Nonsense, she was a free woman, a merry widow, doing as she pleased, no one knew right now where she was and with whom, and she could travel with them wherever she pleased.

Wherever *they* pleased, in fact.

No, wherever *she* pleased, she insisted to herself. After all, she was the driver—she might even consider kidnapping them! The old woman sitting next to her—why old? probably younger than herself—now turned to her all lively and talkative. In fluent Hebrew she told her all about her work in Jerusalem for three families. This family—do you know them? They live in Katamon. And that family—do you know them? They live in Rehavia. And also the judge's family—in Talbiya, surely you know him, he's famous! All good families, and nice to her too; she has been working for them for many years. And even now that she no longer has a permit to enter Jerusalem, let alone a permit to work, even now they don't fire her. Well, so now she walks, sets out at three or four in the morning, crossing hills and valleys, and the pay's not bad at all. She doesn't walk there and back every day; sometimes she stays overnight with a friend in East Jerusalem to avoid the journey. No one waits for her at home anyway, she's a widow, her husband died, God have mercy on him—oh, you too?—and the children are already grown up, all married, good children, thank God. The trouble is she soon won't be able to make it all the way on foot, too bad, they really treat her so well, the people whose homes she's been cleaning all these years, she's like one of the family at the judge's house, they're almost like family.

"Why don't you give us permits?" the talking woman suddenly asked the driving woman, "Maybe you can explain this to me?"

This was a surprise. But because there was no hint of bitterness or powerlessness in the passenger's voice—on the contrary, her whole monologue was filled with the power of life, even joie de vivre —the driving woman answered her simply that no, she could not explain it, and instead of apologizing she burst out laughing.

Why was she laughing?
Perhaps about the maker/keeper of the law in these parts, the famous judge who employed his cleaning woman without a permit? No, there was nothing funny about the thought that he knew nothing of the absurd and even corrupt mechanics of issuing permits and licenses and certificates, an apparatus in whose crooked, ugly cogs this woman and these men were all trapped, crushed, and shredded—he didn't know and he doesn't care.

No, it wasn't this that made her laugh. The laugh was apparently a release from the tension so filled with strangeness that had accumulated in these trips of hers. The driver felt deeply happy now with her four loud passengers.

Light, weightless, was how she felt, as if some huge knot of oppression had disentangled, surged out, and extricated itself from her, before her riders too disentangled themselves, extricating themselves with some effort from her red and too-low-slung Fiesta, took out their bags and looked curiously at Bassem, who came out of his home to greet her. They waved to thank her and held out their hands and shook hers and went on their way.

# The West Bank

# WORKERS

# Someone at the Door

The doorbell rang. Not the loud clang of the intercom but the lighter ring of the apartment doorbell. Well then, perhaps it's a neighbor and she should open. But that morning she didn't feel like getting up from her easy chair in the garden—a woman on her own in an apartment with a garden, sitting and reading a book.

It's God's little acre she's got there. In springtime a vine spreads its young tendrils overhead, and the rosebushes bordering of the lawn are bowed down under the weight of their white and red flowers, and the earthen flowerpots assembled in the corners disappear under the colorful crowns overflowing their rims. The trees have grown high enough to give her, seated in her garden, an enclosed intimacy in the heart of this urban neighborhood, within the stone wall whose top is lined with geraniums sporting their purple and pink and white flowers.

The doorbell rang again, and she got up slowly and went to the door. Through the peephole she saw a striped T-shirt on a man's chest, and she felt the need to hurry: it was uncomfortable, he might sense her presence, the man standing on the other side.

She opened and Tareq faced her, smiling his familiar smile,

part friendly and part cunning, part asking and part demanding. He was dressed neatly, not in the work clothes he wore back when she would see him every day as he supervised the workers who built her apartment building and completed the finishing touches after she had moved in—all the workers from his village. But those days were gone, it had been some time ago, perhaps a year; now the building was finished and entirely inhabited, and its invisible pipes leaked occasionally, and in the underground car park puddles formed, and some of the flagstone facing had broken off the walls. Someone had warily suggested that the hands that built the place had done some sabotage here and there.

"Did I wake you?" Tareq asked, as he always used to ask, for she had never hurried to open the door for him in the morning.

"No," she answered, "I'm working," as she had always answered him back then. Still she opened the door a bit wider and held out a hesitating hand. He entered as he always did, his eyes darting around to detect any changes in her flat, and he took some steps to and fro and was no longer looking at her but at the cell phone he was holding, as if he had some urgent calls to take. She apologized for not inviting him to have a seat because she has no time, she is working right now, and he said he knew and had no intention of disturbing her.

He was disturbing her, though, standing next to the low plaster partition between the dining area and the sitting corner, smiling his smile and telling her what she already knew: he was no longer working for that contractor who had been in charge of this building. She had already heard and known that, she heard that the arrogant and tight-fisted contractor had recently fired them all after fifteen years of working for him, as he decided to employ a subcontractor from the Occupied Territories who would supply the workers himself more easily and cheaply. Still she said: "Oh, really? I didn't know that," in a sympathizing tone which she adopted regularly for such unpleasant, strained circumstances.

"Perhaps you have some work for me?" he asked, or rather murmured.

No, she didn't! She sounded a bit more aggressive: no, how could she have work for him?

"Maybe your friends or something?"

"No, but I'll call you if I hear of anything," she said, and gave no sign of hope that she'd actually do it. "After all, I do have your number."

"No," he said, "it's changed. I have another number now."

She took a piece of paper and wrote down his new number. And waited for him to leave.

But he went on playing around with his cell phone.

Now she realized that his smile was actually embarrassed, perhaps even ashamed, for suddenly he was dependent on her, asking favors, when in the past she was the one to depend on him.

Back then, lord and master in his own domain, he would go up and down the spacious marble-coated stairwell of the large new building—in his work clothes, obviously, but always cleaner and neater than the workers who were his subordinates, for he was a foreman, not a simple worker. He would strut around holding a large bunch of keys and answer ringtones that issued ceaselessly from his cell phone, and answered or didn't answer calls from neighbors upstairs, downstairs, front, and back who needed him, asking him to come and take a look at all kinds of malfunctions and mishaps in their new apartments and make sure to repair them. He really was an important and vital personage at the time, and his name rang out constantly from all corners of the building that gradually became inhabited, echoing Israeli and Anglo-Saxon and Russian accents, and his smile then was in fact a bit arrogant and cunning. Now, as he stood in front of her again after all this time, nothing was left of that smile but a hint at the corner of his mouth, like a cigarette butt one doesn't feel like throwing away.

No, go now, I have no work for you, she said decidedly but voicelessly, to herself.

For she wanted Tareq to get lost, whether because in all those months he had worked here she never really grew to like him, unlike some of the other workers, whom she befriended and thanks to whom she enjoyed her wonderful relationship with Amal and her daughters, or because she felt extremely uncomfortable in this kind of situation in which she had found herself occasionally—and still finds herself time and again—in her meetings and conversations with Palestinian people of West Bank villages.

Yes, especially because she felt uncomfortable, for she wished to get back to her morning calm, to the shady garden and the padded wicker chair and matching small wicker table and her book and her cup of coffee. She did not offer to make him a cup of coffee, she did not even offer him a glass of cool water on this hot day.

He's going, he said, he really doesn't want to disturb her, but just a minute: maybe she could write a letter to the army for two friends of his who have applied and are not being issued magnetic cards or an entry permit or a work permit, write the army or the Civil Administration or the Shabak (General Security Services)—as she had often done in the past, as other Israelis, especially Israeli women, still often do, in fact—to look into what the authorities have on them. He knows they're clean, they've never done a thing.

Another moment and she would have told him that it's too bad they never did anything, she wished they finally would—smartass that she was.

"No, I can't," she said. "Look, the rules have changed." Suddenly she found herself in the role of a patient clerk at the Civil Administration offices or the army or god knows what the hell, and she gave him a lecture about the new rules that are now in force, rules she had received in writing just lately, with explanations, from a group of volunteer women who handle this issue with immeasurable dedication and diligence, trying, sometimes even successfully, to help the Palestinian workers who apply and are not issued permits to work in Israel.

Well, according to these rules one should first of all distinguish between the various types of permit:

permit to work in Israel
permit to work in Israeli settlements in the Occupied Territories
permit to enter Israel on business
permit to enter the seam-line zone for farming purposes
permit to travel during closure
permit to enter Israel to reach a hospital . . .

This she read him aloud from the pages she had brought from another room and spread out on the wooden shelf at the top of the plaster partition. Her eyes scanned the precise instructions for issuing a "permit to enter Israel on business" that differentiated in large subheadings between "merchants 30 years old or older who are fathers to children" and "merchants under 30, or over 30 but without children." "In most areas," the document stipulated, "applicants may be issued permits only through the Trade Bureaus. In areas where the merchant may apply for a permit on his own, he must go to the DCO [District Coordinating Office] with all the necessary documents and apply. If the permit is to be issued, the merchant will be instructed to have a magnetic card made. If a permit is not issuable because the applicant is security-blacklisted, the Trade Bureaus may fill out his form and hand it in at the place where permit applications are turned in. Since the Trade Bureau personnel are not fluent in Hebrew, the merchant may be equipped with a form that has already been filled out, and he must then turn it in with all the necessary documents and the Trade Bureaus will do it for him. In the 'notes' section of the form the applicant's family status should be mentioned, as well as the type of business and whether he has a police or security record. If the applicant is married to an Israeli citizen or resident of Israel and their children are registered in her ID, proof must be given that he has children . . ."

But Tareq was interested in a work permit, naturally, both in Israel and in the settlements, and not a permit for trade purposes: he had nothing to trade.

All right, she said, listen, about work permits it says here: "Workers 30 years old or older and fathers of children . . . For workers under 30 or over 30 but without children the procedure is the same, but only employers in the settlements or in the seam-line zone are acceptable . . ."

She reached the point where the writers of the document noted that workers were no longer to file application letters, and this she read to Tareq with a sense of mean relief. Yes, she was definitely aware of the meanness in her relief—relief for getting rid of the need to meet the requests she is constantly faced with to write application letters to the Civil Administration or army authorities or Shabak or DCO or staff officer or god knows what despicable authorities end up receiving those letters and handling or not handling them.

"No, it says here they no longer send letters," she explained without hesitation. "The worker needs to find an Israeli employer, and the employer must try to get him a permit. If the employer doesn't manage to get a permit for him because he is security-denied—in other words, the worker is blacklisted by the Shabak or police," she recited, "the employer must fill out a form and send it to the Employment Staff Officer at the Civil Administration offices in Beit El, a certain Yitzhak Levi. And if the employer finds it difficult to fill out the form, we are willing to do it with him." She quoted for Tareq what the volunteers had written in this document, and hoped she would never be asked to sit with some employer and fill out forms.

"If all these procedures fail," she continued reading—and all that time they stood by the plaster partition, she and Tareq—"one might appeal to the Supreme Court. There is a woman lawyer who does this for a fee of only a few hundred shekels, and she comes to meet the applicants on certain days of the week.

"Would you like to know when and where? Would you like me to give you a form? You could photocopy it and pass it on to your friends. Does that work for you?" she asked Tareq, now with great willingness.

But that day Tareq didn't want to know where, nor did he want to take a form from her. He thanked her politely and took off, and never returned.

# The Passengers in Car Trunks

Back in the days when the Palestinian workers who built her apartment building in the Jerusalem neighborhood of Beit Ha-Kerem were still giving the building its finishing touches—the third millennium was then five years old, and she had moved there from her flat in the Katamon neighborhood in order to have a private garden—she went down one day to the spacious car park and storage basement to fetch something from her storage space. And there she saw one of her neighbors with an unfamiliar worker, and for some reason she asked who that worker was and from where, just out of curiosity and her tendency to be friendly with everyone at her new dwelling.

The neighbor hesitated for a moment and then told her, lowering his voice, that he wished to make some renovations in his storage space, work that was beyond what the regular workers did, so he had asked them whether any of them knew a renovator who could do the job. One of the workers said his brother was unemployed and looking for work. When the neighbor suggested the worker bring his unemployed brother along, the worker told him that his brother did not have a permit to enter Israel.

"So I went there with my car and he got into the trunk and that's how I brought him here . . ." said the neighbor.

She did not respond.

"What, aren't they human beings?" asked the neighbor.

She did not respond.

That woman sometimes has too many things to say, and at other times, dammit, she stays silent even if she knows it's necessary, even urgent, to say something.

"What are these people supposed to live on? Tell me!" The neighbor was agitated, having become a smuggler-employer.

She responded: she promised him not to tell anyone that he'd smuggled a worker in the trunk of his car.

Later she came to understand that secrets are secrets but not for those who wish to know. Many workers are smuggled this way, and there are even set fees: a thin boy pays his smuggler seventy or eighty shekels, a heavy man ninety.

She believes, or would like to believe at least, that the worker she saw was transported in the trunk free of charge.

# The Walkers

One Saturday night, late, she drove her red Ford Fiesta down the alleys of a Palestinian village in Area B—or perhaps A or C. The third millennium was already ten years old, she was not on her own this time, a local man was with her. With that man, in his midlife and father of a large family, she had already had such dramatic experiences—she wouldn't want to recount them all—that they had become close friends. Not necessarily a spiritual or emotional closeness. Rather, circumstances had taught them to know each other very well in all kinds of situations and cooperate like a well-knit team: this too is a way for friendship to be forged.

Despite the hour, the village was bustling with life. Private cars and taxis and transit vans inched down the streets, while others were parked anywhere possible; dozens of people sat on chairs at house doorways and shops and improvised cafés, or on the pavement or the ground, and smoked cigarettes and drank black coffee from small paper cups, poured for them by boys and children from thermos bottles for one shekel. This bustle was there for anyone to see, as were the armed soldiers who stood next to their military vehicles or sat inside them at the entrances to the village and at various spots along its streets.

The woman too stood out a bit in that man's world, different from everyone and foreign to them, but not to her companion, who even insisted on introducing her to some of the people: an Israeli, a Jew, who wishes to "see the situation here." The two of them made their way in her car through the village and onto a side road winding through a darkness pierced only imperfectly by the car's headlights, descending in sharp bends into one of the ravines at the foot of the village.

The road was very narrow. Soon along its sides, from within the darkness of low clumps of trees and bushes, cigarette tips and small squares of light from cell phones began to appear like fireflies. Then figures suddenly emerged by the roadside, three or four, and when the woman and her friend stopped and got out of the car they were already surrounded by about fifteen men, not exactly young—in the car headlights she saw some gray hair and lined faces. Their clothes were neat and clean, they were on their way to work: in Tel Aviv, in Bnei Brak, in Ashkelon, and even in the northern city of Haifa. They came out of Hebron and its surroundings, Bethlehem and its surroundings, and many of them had left their homes very early that morning in faraway Nablus and Jenin in order to reach this part of the Jerusalem hills where the Separation Barrier had not yet been erected.

When the woman and her companion met this group, its members were about to move away from the road and vanish among the bushes and trees. Indeed they had neither the time nor the patience for conversation; they hurried to take their leave. The woman was also in a hurry: she took a pair of walking shoes out of her car, more suitable for a long walk than the sandals she was wearing. She meant to join them.

But suddenly the plan changed, another group arrived from

below, and one of its members said the army was waiting up on the other side of the ravine. He said the soldiers had arrested some of the workers who had crossed the ravine and almost made it to the road where Israeli cars belonging to their employers or their messengers waited to collect them on the other side of the checkpoint and drive them an hour or two or three to Tel Aviv or Bnei Brak or Ashkelon or Haifa. They had very nearly made it—but were caught. The bearers of this bad news witnessed this in time to escape and turn back.

Now the men were in no hurry to go anywhere, had all become persons with time on their hands, Time to tell their stories, because they would no longer proceed to their workplaces, not for the next few hours anyway.

Most of them worked in Israel in construction or renovation jobs, they said, but had no permits. Many of them were "blacklisted," meaning they were among the hundreds of thousands of Palestinians who for years have been denied entry into Israel. Some of them were "Shabak-blacklisted" and others "police-blacklisted"—their terms. They were deemed dangerous persons, threats to the security of the State of Israel, and therefore they were to remain in their places, they and the explosives and knives they might be carrying.

What they *were* carrying was backpacks, not just plastic bags but proper backpacks, clean and neat like their clothing. In the backpacks were changes of clothes and toilet articles to permit them to stay a week or two, even a month, at or near their workplaces. There was no livelihood to be earned in their own communities, and they absolutely had to feed their families. Their homes were full of babies and young children who needed to be clothed and raised and sent to school and then university. Yes, even to the university. In fact most university students in the

West Bank have no jobs waiting for them after they graduate—
but who knows, perhaps the situation will change and the next
generation will have a better life. In the meantime a day of
work in their communities, if work is to be had, brings in about
60 shekels. The wages for a workday in Israel—and there is usually work to be had in Israel—are about 150–200 shekels. And
so they cross over by the thousands, probably tens of thousands.

First they ride cars from their own towns and villages
throughout the West Bank, eight or nine workers in a normal-
sized car. Twenty or more crowd into a transit van, crushed together, one on top of the other. Then they walk an hour or two
on foot, bypassing checkpoints; then they crowd once more
into cars that await them at designated spots inside Israel. Others arrive on foot at certain places in Jerusalem or its outskirts
and proceed by public transportation, blending in among other
passengers. To make this possible they mind their appearance,
making sure to dress neatly and respectably, their faces clean-
shaven.

And why are they blacklisted? Some of them guess it's because of a brother doing jail time, or a cousin killed by the army,
leading the Israeli authorities to fear acts of revenge. Some of
them have police records for unpaid fines; or they paid their
fines but the closing of their file does not yet register on the
computer screen at the DCO that issues permits. Others, by
the hundreds or thousands, have no idea why they are blacklisted: they have already knocked on the doors of the DCO and
the Shabak, lined the pockets of attorneys, but no reason has
come to light. And so they keep returning and undertake the
dangerous crossing at sites where the Barrier has not yet been
completed. Some were caught but managed to kick loose and
run; some were arrested, imprisoned, released, and are on the

move again; from time to time someone gets shot, wounded, even killed, but most of them arrive safely at their workplaces.

And there they are defined—these people are constantly defined—as "illegal aliens." They can be seen at construction sites, sometimes at neighborhood grocery stores, in stained and dusty work clothes, unshaven after long days of work and nights of sleep in impossible conditions, for they can't undertake this exhausting, dangerous, and difficult journey, this expensive—about 200 shekels each way—journey, on a daily basis, so they stay overnight in Israel, in towns and villages, anywhere they can, and return home once every week or two, or once a month. In Israel they build and renovate buildings and apartments.

In that night journey of hers—she later made others like it—she could see they were tired, but they were still neat and tidy. Their looks and their speech did not suggest people who were humiliated and oppressed. This was their struggle for survival, and they wished to survive, to live; come what may, they would put food on the table in their homes full of babies. Nearly all of them spoke fluent Hebrew. "I walk with my nose up, you hear," said one man, pushing the tip of his nose up with a finger. "I'm a proud man. I'm proud to be feeding my children."

Had she recorded all the personal survival stories she heard on those Saturday nights, she wouldn't have known how to articulate them. Was it the powerlessness of words? Her shame? Her rage? She wished she could say. But she was not allowed to record anyone anyway and not even to write things down. For the circumstances did not permit absolute trust—neither her purpose of political documentation, which she made as clear as she could to her interlocutors, nor she herself, as an Israeli Jewish woman, could be trusted absolutely.

That night, when she passed that spot on the road again a few hours later, the people she had spoken with at the roadside were no longer there. They might have managed to bypass the checkpoint and proceed to their workplaces, others might have gone back home to rest and try again the next day, and perhaps others found shelter overnight with friends, in mosques, in hidden corners of the village, under a tree or by a wall.

The workers had been there and now they were gone. But the soldiers were still present: now and then a foot patrol went by, here and there stood army jeeps with their lights out, here and there soldiers entered a house to arrest someone in the dead of night. That's how it is in these villages—the soldiers are present night and day. So they are in the know: the dozens of workers she saw that night, waiting for their moment to cross over to Israel, the soldiers saw them too.

The security official of Beitar Ilit settlement with whom she spoke the next morning in his office was aware of them as well. "You should see what went on here last night," he said after proudly describing the settlement's security arrangements, which were much more responsible and humane, in his opinion, than elsewhere.

"I did see," she told him. "And what do you make of it?"

"That's the way it is all the time." He shrugged. "Usually we turn a blind eye and everyone gets through. You want to know something? Yesterday there was an operation, that's all. A few were arrested, just so people won't think they can enter Israel so easily, so they won't take it for granted. This way their lives are made a bit more difficult. And you want to know something else? By about 1:30 a.m. the operation was over and most of them could get through."

"And tomorrow?" she asked.

"Tomorrow there won't be any operation, I'm sure. I think you can tell that to your friends: they can go right ahead and come in, nothing will happen to them." That's how he joked with her, and he wanted her to know much more, "things those spoiled Tel Avivians don't know," he said.

And she listened to him, that spoiled Jerusalemite. She did know these things very well, for she had been documenting them for years, and still she listened to him, for it was important and interesting for her to hear them explicitly from him, a man of public duty, a "security official." He told her about an elaborate trade in permits to enter Israel that flourishes and is highly lucrative. When Israeli employers and contractors purchase entry permits for workers from the employment services, they order more permits than the number of workers they really need; they sell the remainder to contractors in the Occupied Territories who in turn sell them to workers at exorbitant prices.

"Want to know their price?" he asked, and was visibly disappointed when she replied, "No, I already know."

Yes, she knew: 1,800 shekels at least, and if it's a "zero-zero" permit—that is, for both day and night—then much more. The buyers of these permits crowd along with the "kosher" permit holders in that crushing line between the barbed-wire fences of the checkpoints like livestock on their way to the corral, to the cowshed, to the sheep pen. But the contractor who confirms with his signature that he employs them—that is, he knows them and is responsible for their comings and goings inside Israel—has never seen them and will never see them. Even the phone numbers written on these traded permits might be fictitious. This she witnessed herself that day with the help of a fellow who showed her such a document.

"Here, I'm calling," he said, then dialed and let her listen.

"The number you have dialed is not connected," the recording informed her, short and to the point. The guy had paid 2,200 shekels for this permit, which was even printed with a semblance of formality, and the day she met this buyer he still had another four days left to spend in Israel, according to the dates stipulated on the document, time in which to do as he pleased from 5 a.m. until 7 p.m. To blow himself up and blow others up and stab and run people over.

"What would I feel like doing in his stead?" the woman wondered. And she answered herself: "But I don't need to survive—he does." And the simple truth was that he felt like working, that fellow, but he had not found work lately. If he did find work, he'd buy a new permit from someone else, he told her.

Everyone knows where they can be bought, but not everyone can afford it—most of them don't have the money. And so they undertake that awful trip across the hills, more awful even than the crowding and the humiliation at the checkpoints, and certainly more dangerous.

# Captured

Once the woman received a phone call from the sister of two of the workers who walk to their workplace from somewhere else in the West Bank. She told her that these two brothers had been caught at their workplace inside Israel and arrested. "Perhaps you could help us find out where they're being held?" she asked. The woman could. "Perhaps you could find four Jews to post bail for my brother at the Ashqelon court?" she asked the woman the next day. The woman couldn't.

Another two days went by, and one of the brothers, let's call him Rami, was released pending his scheduled trial. "Perhaps," the sister said to the woman on behalf of the brother who remained in jail, let's call him 'Alaa, "you could deposit some money on his behalf in the prison canteen account through the Israel Postal Bank—money for cigarettes?" The woman could, and did.

"Perhaps you could deposit 3,000 shekels in 'Alaa's canteen account?" the sister asked the next day as she called, adding immediately: "We'll pay you back!"

"So much money?" the woman wondered. "What for?"

"Because my brother needs to pay the fine imposed on him last time he was caught without a permit," the sister explained.

"That fine, which was suspended, now goes into effect. If he doesn't pay it, he will remain in jail for two months before trial on account of being caught as an illegal alien now. If he pays, he gets released like Rami."

This was the sister's explanation, and she asked again: "Can you?" Perhaps she even stated: You can.

The woman deliberated for a moment, and then she said she could—why not, actually? She had already deposited money for cigarettes in the prisoner's canteen account. She went again to the same neighborhood branch of the Postal Bank, tore off a number stub from the red device at the entrance, and waited for her number in line to finally appear on the screen. When it did, she approached the window, handed the money to the clerk—the same one who had served her the day before—and from a note she held, read out again the long line of digits of the canteen account. He typed it as she read, typed in the amount, and the computer screen announced that the sum was too large: so much money cannot be deposited in a prisoner's canteen account. That's it, nothing can be done, the clerk said. The clerk was sorry that she'd waited so long in line for nothing.

She stepped aside and called Rami to consult with him, but the brother was helpless—he only knew that the time for paying the fine would be up in two days.

The woman sat down on the red metal bench inside the Israel Post branch, racked her brain, and decided to call the prison where 'Alaa was being held. First she called the Israel Prison Service, where she was answered by an automatic call distributor that guided her from one prison to another—Shita (in Hebrew: mimosa), Hadarim (citrus trees and fruit), Nitzan (blossom), Ohalei Keidar (biblical appellation of nomads' black goat-wool tents), each name more pastoral than the previous—

until she finally reached the right one: Shiqma (sycamore tree) Prison in Ashqelon. But the secretary who answered told her that the prisoner she was looking for was no longer there; he had been moved to Damoun Prison.

Back to the automatic call distributor: she pressed the number of the Damoun Prison on Mount Carmel and was answered by a recorded announcement that this prison did not receive visitors—and then the line went silent. She again called Shiqma Prison, where she already knew the secretary, and the secretary advised her to try the court system, perhaps they'd know what was to be done when a fine needed to be paid. The woman called the court system and was directed and redirected until she finally got a human response, and the secretary who answered suggested she might try the military court system. The woman called the military court system, where a human responder looked for the prisoner's ID in his lists and no such prisoner was found there, whereupon he directed her once again to the civilian court system.

She listened again to the recording of the call distributor, and this time chose to press the number of the information center of the Government Law Enforcement and Collection System: who if not these people would know how to pay fines? And indeed through this center she was directed to an automated response that suggested she could pay various kinds of debts through this channel, debts that were specified one by one, and she had only to choose, but a fine imposed on an illegal alien was not among them.

She returned to the national information center of the court system and from there followed the numbers from court to court, until she got to the Ashqelon Magistrate Court in the home city of Shiqma Prison, the first place where her "client" was detained—for it was reasonable to assume that that was also where the arrest warrant for her "client" was issued.

"Her client," then. By now the woman had granted him that title as she thought about it. In a place where there are no attorneys, strive to be one. Being flippant was enjoyable, and there *was* a touch of logic, for 'Alaa now really needed an attorney, but since he had no money to pay one, there was no attorney.

From the Ashqelon Magistrate Court she was sent to the neighboring Ashdod Magistrate Court, as it turned out that 'Alaa had been tried there. Well, it's not that far, the woman muttered to herself as if she were driving rather than talking on the phone. And indeed a secretary there finally told her that this was the right place and that she could come to her and get the voucher with which the fine could be paid—and without which it could not be paid.

"I live in Jerusalem," the woman told her. "Could that voucher be faxed to me?"

"No," the secretary answered her adamantly, "the Postal Bank will not receive payment by fax."

"Wait just a minute, please! I'll ask the clerk, don't hang up," the woman pleaded and began to stumble to the counter, one hand holding the phone to her ear and the other desperately crushing the thick wad of notes with the multitude of phone numbers she had accumulated before reaching the right number,

"I'm waiting—what's the matter with you, why are you so worried?" the secretary's voice wondered.

"There, you hear?" the woman said to her from the counter. "The clerk says I can pay by fax, as long as the data is clearly written. I'll give you the fax number of this postal branch in a moment." But the clerk who heard her said that the fax machine at that Israel Post branch had been out of order since that morning; he even tried it on the spot to make sure. Out of order—that's it, nothing to do about it, he was sorry for her, again.

The woman then gave the secretary her home fax number and went home, and there the fax was already waiting for her as promised, the page from the Ashdod Magistrate Court with the voucher number, the sum to be paid, and the debtor details. She returned to the post branch.

"You could have driven to Ashdod and back by now," the postal clerk joked with her. Curious, he took a peek at the name and the sum, and asked: "What has this guy done, to be fined so steeply?"

"This guy went to work in Israel without a permit," the woman answered him. "He has to support his family—you can understand that, can't you?"

The clerk may have understood this, but he only raised his eyebrows, inserted the voucher into the machine, typed in the sum, stamped the payment stub, handed it back to her, and took leave wishing her "good tidings."

Whether he really meant it or not, his good wishes did materialize: brother 'Alaa was released upon the payment of his fine, and he returned home.

"Maybe you can help me get back my personal effects that were taken from me when I was jailed in Ashqelon and have not been returned?" 'Alaa asked the woman a few days after his release. "I have the form that lists them."

In order to get the form from 'Alaa, and finally meet both brothers in person—and also because she likes these drives on her own in the West Bank, for the landscape is nearly as beau-

tiful as in Tuscany—the woman drove to the family's town of
residence a few days later. In her red Ford Fiesta she passed the
red road sign forbidding her to enter "Area A, the Palestinian
Authority territory." She drove slowly, gazing curiously at the
streets and shops and people; then with the brothers she had
juice and coffee and tea and munched some wafers and smoked
a few cigarettes, and 'Alaa handed her the form—a small slip
of yellow paper, ragged and wrinkled, with the Israel Prison
Service insignia at the top and the heading "Specification of
the personal effects and money belonging to the prisoner/
detainee." She read him the list, scribbled in Hebrew:

1. Cash: 300 NIS
2. Cell phone
3. Brown wallet
4. Cell phone case

The list was correct, 'Alaa confirmed, but unfortunately for
him the prison storage was closed at the time of his release, too
early and perhaps too late, and the items remained there. He
was told he could come any other day, present the form, and
receive them. But how could he come if he was forbidden to
enter Israel?

This question was later directed in writing to a Prison Service
spokesperson, and he answered it precisely as follows: "In case
the person in question, resident of the Territories, is released
there directly from the court or at a late time of day according
to the release order, he will be told that his belongings will be
transferred to the Crossings Administration at the checkpoint
nearest his dwelling in order for him to receive them on the
spot. The Prison Service explains and clarifies this to the pris-

oner prior to his release and confirms the transfer of all of the items wholly and inclusively."

Good. The trouble is that in 'Alaa's case a mistake was made and he was told very clearly that his things would be returned to him at the offices of the Red Cross. But there he was told very clearly that not the Red Cross but rather the Palestinian Authority was in charge of the matter. Then at the PA offices he was told very clearly that his things might reach them in about ten months.

The trouble—yet more trouble—is that his ID was not returned to him either, and ten months without an ID is a long time, very long. By law one must carry upon one's person an identifying document wherever one goes. And 'Alaa now had no document attesting to his identity, the legality of which was always doubtful under his present life circumstances—actually it had been tenuous from the day he was born.

It came to pass that he thought, after a while, of traveling to Ramallah to run some errands and perhaps have a bit of fun, as he was now a free person but unemployed, with plenty of time on his hands. He seated himself in a shared taxicab, which brought him to the crossing-and-inspection point commonly known as the "Container Checkpoint" on Wadi A-Nar Road, separating the southern part of the West Bank from the northern part. This checkpoint is meant only for Palestinians, and they do not need permits to cross it, but they do need to be inspected, and the soldiers checked and discovered that 'Alaa had only a very vague record of his own identity: "Confirmation of a Prisoner's Term in Jail." This document, said the soldiers, is valid only for three days after the prisoner's release from prison. So how is it that nearly a month has gone by and he is walking through the land in the length of it and in the breadth of it with this miserable slip of paper?

Still, fortune smiled on 'Alaa, and the soldiers allowed him
to proceed north. In Ramallah he did what he had meant to
do, and he returned safely to his town in the southern West
Bank, an area so much more impoverished and depressed than
its northern counterpart.

Not many days passed by and fortune smiled upon him
again, in a much more important matter: contrary to the statement by the Prison Service spokesperson, it turned out that
said service could not confirm "transfer of the prisoner's items
wholly and inclusively" anywhere, and the items—the money,
wallet, and cell phone, as well as the ID—were wholly and inclusively held at Shiqma Prison in Ashqelon. Thus one month
and three days after his release, and upon presentation of the
yellow slip of paper plus a power of attorney signed by 'Alaa,
for which a woman had traveled to his town—this time a different woman, who also violated the order forbidding entry
there—wallet, phone, and ID were handed to this woman, who
promptly returned them to their owner.


This minor episode had a happy ending, then, but the larger
was not yet over. After a while the two brothers stood trial and
were convicted. A transcript of the proceedings shows how the
female judge deliberated: On the one hand she believed they,
like many others, were motivated by economic need to commit
the deeds for which they were being prosecuted. On the other
hand, she believed that one must take into consideration the
"security aspect resulting from the severe security situation that
the State of Israel faces and its need to protect its borders from
those coming to inflict harm." She therefore sought balance
in her verdict, and to the best of her judgment found it: "The

need to struggle against unlawful entry and sojourn is understandable. However, dire need and search of livelihood is also understood. Balance is the name of the legal objective." She sentenced the two as follows: 'Alaa, who had been caught and convicted twice before, was sentenced to a month in jail plus a fine of 3,000 shekels, plus a three-year suspended sentence of six months in jail and a fine of 12,000 shekels. Rami, with his "totally clean record," was given a three-year suspended sentence of five months in jail and a 4,000-shekel fine.

In fact, this is what such legal balance looks like: in the Hebrew city where the two had been employed, thousands of workers defined as "illegal aliens" still work, in spite of the State of Israel's need to struggle against their unlawful entry and sojourn in order to defend its borders. Meanwhile in the town where the two brothers reside there is now one more household, theirs, with fourteen persons—parents and children and parents of parents—who have nothing to live on. Literally nothing. For in this town and its surroundings there are not enough employers.

"We're sorry for what we did," the two defendants stated at their trial. But these words of theirs quoted in the court transcript do not tally with the end of the statement: "We only came to work." Obviously the two regretted one thing only: having been caught (and hence having to live in fear of gambling away their freedom and thousands of shekels which they do not possess). But this regret was so great, and the lack of options so desperate, that for the woman who followed this story it was obvious that it was not at all over—they would leave again at the crack of dawn on the dangerous trek across hills and valleys toward the openings in the fence, and either cross or be caught.

# Her Own Passenger in the Car Trunk

The third millennium moved on: it was already fifteen years old, and the woman seventy-one. And then one bright day, while stepping up and down the Cross-Trainer at the gym in sweaty determination, she was approached by her ophthalmologist, who was also a member of that gym. In the easygoing quiet politeness typical of those frequenting the place, he told her: "When you're done, there's something I want to ask you."

When she was done, he noticed and immediately got off an identical machine and came toward her. They moved to one side, by the gymnastics ladder. "This morning an electrician was working at my place," he began, "an excellent electrician—I employ him regularly." She looked at him, wondering, and he hurried to explain: "You are the person to ask," he said. "This electrician comes from Bethlehem, and after all you hang out there in the Territories and always know what's wrong."

"Yes," she answered.

Well, she doesn't always know, but even when she knows and wishes to share some of this information with him on her visits to his clinic, he has listened impatiently and skeptically and almost always has had some disgruntled response.

This she kept to herself.

"So perhaps you know," he went on, "whether it's true what my electrician told me: that his employer, who now practically never employs him, charges him 2,000 shekels a month for the permit to enter Israel which he obtains for him although he doesn't employ him anymore. What is the guy paying so much money for? Maybe you can tell me?"

Obviously he was suspecting some flaw in the proper order of things, maybe even total disorder.

"Maybe there is even corruption?" he said, wrinkling his brow.

"Yes, maybe. Yes, perhaps even corruption. Who would have believed it?" She couldn't help but tease him.

But she had no answer to the specific question he had asked. For the truth is that by this time her senses had gone a bit dull from all the darkness she has seen over the years in all those "proper orders"—yes, orders—that control the West Bank, and for some time now she had not heeded that particular shade of gray: trading and black-marketing entry permits for Palestinians. Perhaps she even assumed that this plague had vanished by now.

Plague? Several years earlier some good women had objected when she wanted to write about this for the newspaper. After all, many workers benefit from the trade in permits, and without it they could not make a living, so you had better not write—let it go.

And she let it go. After all, what good would it do?

Now, by the gymnastics ladder in the gym, she recalled this and nervously waved her hand. She waved it as if trying to shoo away the tiny but insistent fly that almost always pestered her—it or its relatives—at a certain point along the route of her regular bike ride in the Jerusalem hills. It would easily escape her waving hand until she would nearly lose her balance, and again and again it would manage to set its six delicate and tickling legs right on her face, sticky from the sweet snack she had eaten during a break under a tree or on a rock. But in the gym the bikes do not move in space no matter how hard their riders pedal, and there are no flies and no need to wave one's hands.

"I don't know what he's paying for," she answered her ophthalmologist reluctantly. "But it is highly likely—I've heard such stories before. There's apparently some administration or government office that requires a payment, and there are employers who add to that sum and pocket the difference."

"Really?" He was genuinely amazed. "If that's so, then this is corruption, clear corruption! Could you find out? But if you do, don't write in the paper about the Occupation again, only about corruption. After all, that's what matters here, so your piece will be much more effective if you stick to that."

She promised him to look into it. This was the beginning of a short chain of coincidences, a chain that became the last straw . . .

The next day an unfamiliar woman called her, said her name, known to her from literary circles, and told her in an agitated voice that she has lately returned from a long stay abroad and doesn't understand what's going on now. The Arab worker who has been renovating her place has asked if she knows anyone else who can give him work, urgently, because he cannot afford to pay the 2,200 shekels to the person from whom he gets his entry permit although the man no longer employs him.

"What is this?" the caller asked angrily, adding that she was so upset by the man's distress that she had found herself obliged to have him stay overnight at her home as long as he was working there in order to save him the daily travel expenses to and from his village. Perhaps she knew—she probably didn't—that this meant she was committing the offense of harboring an illegal alien. At any rate she hurriedly ended the conversation once she realized that she was wasting her time: "the tireless pro-Palestinian activist," as she defined the woman incorrectly, could not do anything. The call's recipient had no reasonable answer, no in with the authorities to help that worker who had managed to land on a tender spot in the conscience of the caller.

"What is this?" the woman asked herself and others a few days later. It was a scorching summer Saturday, and she was sitting in the living room of a Palestinian family with whom she'd been friends for years now. They had just told her—what a coincidence—that one of their sons wished to work in Israel during his summer holidays but had no entry permit, and he was deliberating whether to purchase one for 1,800 shekels, a steep sum for him.

Was she really playing dumb, asking "What is this?" Was she really still asking? She knew, after all. But the family members flooded her with details and even competed over who would shock her more: the elder daughter told about a fellow who paid 2,500, and her younger sister said there were now guys who demanded 3,000.

"Not true." The woman couldn't help herself and urged that they be precise: "No need to exaggerate—it's already bad enough."

"It's true!" said the girl defiantly and turned to her mother, naming some uncle or cousin. "That's what he told us, right?"

The mother didn't bother to answer. True or not, precise or not, what did it matter? The situation is really bad—that's what matters. And then the student son mentioned the possibility of smuggling himself in a car trunk—that only cost 100 or 120.

These prices too have risen in the meantime.

Did she just imagine the son giving her a hopeful look?

This family gathered around her on that Saturday—a father, a mother, two octogenarian grandparents whose health was declining, and six children—are dependent for their daily bread mostly on the plot of ground around their home. They skillfully grow vegetables and vines and fruit trees, mostly for domestic consumption and some for sale. The father tried to cultivate some produce in greenhouses but failed. She still remembers purchasing pepper plants for him at an Israeli nursery, because he thought the Israeli nurseries were better and fairer than the ones in the West Bank. The peppers did thrive, but then there was very little demand, for it happened that all the greenhouse owners in the area grew peppers in that season. The income barely covered expenses. The next season brought drought, so no income whatsoever.

Over a period of months she saw the plastic sheets covering the greenhouses gradually drooping away from the rods and the rods themselves going awry and then bending down—until the entire greenhouse had collapsed flat on the ground. Then its dismembered parts must have been collected and removed, for only barren ground remained. Some decades ago all the villagers around here had been farmers, sons of farmers. No longer. Perhaps inexorable urbanization would have changed the lives of the villagers even without the Israeli military takeover, but the large urban settlements that were erected and built during this time before their very eyes, and hers, on land confiscated from them—and whose construction supplied them with not-so-bad work and livelihood for quite a while—were now inhabited not by them but by Israeli citizens.

Either way, for some years the father of this family has usually been unemployed. Still his children have accomplished quite a bit in the meantime—it was always a riddle for her how despite the hardship and the poverty, these children grow up well here. They all go to school, and two older ones, a boy and a girl, are attending college.

The girl had the forethought to begin hairdresser training before registering for college, and now she is both a college student and a professional hairdresser—two days a week she studies accounting and three days she works at a salon. Eventually she may open her own salon and do her own accounting. Her chances are much better than those of her brother, who is studying some sort of computer science. His fate is likely to be that of many young adults in the West Bank, who have graduated college or university and are now jobless. Or they renovate homes in settlements and inside Israel. The sister, on the other hand, is already earning rather well, for there are certain kinds of businesses that do flourish in the West Bank, and one of them is hairdressing.

The woman wondered about this as she saw the heads of

women and girls all covered: not a single hair would escape
the fabric and matching kerchief tightly covering their heads.
Gone were the days when women walked around the villages
bareheaded. Even in the cities increasing numbers of women
covered their heads now. But hairdresser salons were still flour-
ishing. How come?

She didn't find an answer to this except at weddings. But
there the answer was impressive indeed! Such craftsmanship—
braiding and weaving and raising and straightening and curl-
ing and waving, in so many shades—in the hairstyles on the
small dance floors where women danced crowded against each
other in festive dresses and jewelry, literally embodying what
the prophet had said about Jerusalem: "I clothed thee also with
broidered work, and shod thee with badgers' skin, and I girded
thee about with fine linen, and I covered thee with silk. I decked
thee also with ornaments, and I put bracelets upon thy hands,
and a chain on thy neck. And I put a jewel on thy forehead, and
earrings in thine ears, and a beautiful crown upon thine head"
(Ezekiel 16:10–13).


Another week or two went by after that visit at the home of the
hairdresser-student's family, and the woman couldn't make up
her mind. Was she only imagining that the student son who
dismissed the possibility of buying an entry permit to Israel had
looked at her hopefully when he spoke of perhaps smuggling
himself in a car trunk? She was afraid to smuggle this young fellow who wished to improve his life—where might he be forced
to look for work, and mightn't he rather end up looking for a
good time? But why not his father? After all, she would like to
have the apartment that she intends to rent out be repainted.

The father had already painted this same apartment to her satisfaction some years back—why not have him repaint it now?

Soon the decision was made: yes, this would be her answer
to the ophthalmologist, regardless of whether she'd let him in
on it—and she went to see the Palestinian family again.


"I have work for you." She told the father almost as soon as she
arrived so as to keep from changing her mind. And thus she
also finally gave him a positive answer to the question he had
long ago given up asking. She told him what the work was and
promised a generous wage. His face brightened. He hurried to
say that money was not the issue; the main thing was that she'd
be satisfied: "What wouldn't I do for you—you know what you
mean to us!"

That is what he said, and she nodded. She was no longer
embarrassed by these statements—such was the relationship
here, not among equals, yet still humane and warm and even
wonderful because of the special way she and the family have
nurtured it for so many years despite bad times. But she is embarrassed when the father—always looking for a way to open
wider a door that is opened only to him, and only slightly—
suggests that his son come along.

"No." She was annoyed. "The flat is very small. You know
it—there's only work enough for one person." She was aware
that the son would use any such opportunity to look for a new
job. The father sighed and gave in, and they set a date soon
when she would come to fetch him.

They did not discuss how exactly they meant to enter Jerusalem together.

Who cares? The red Ford Fiesta would break barriers, uproot

rods and poles at checkpoints, crawl upon its belly through the black darkness of tunnels, leap over bridges, grow wings and fly in the blue skies stretched over it all. "'Even through walls bloweth my free breath,' spoke Zarathustra," spoke she, and she felt glad.

But she already knew that before setting out to pick him up, she'd empty her car trunk.

On the appointed day she rose early, threw her stuff on the front seat of the car, went around to the rear, and opened the trunk. What a disaster! How could she have put off this task to the last minute? There were bottles both empty and filled with drink for people, bottles both empty and filled with drink for cars, for cooling the engine in the summer heat and for anti-freezing its fluid in the winter cold and for washing the windshield and for enriching fuel, and there was the huge gray seat cover that served Momo the dog when she sat in the backseat, and there was a safety harness for the dog, and bowls and dishes and cups and a folding chair and clothes and books for leisure time and for various emergencies.

All of which now had to be removed.

First things were put aside and sorted in an orderly fashion. Then they were nervously thrown every which way, her tension increasing in view of the relatively small area actually freed and the watch hands ticking on and on, and finally the things were gathered again and packed messily, tearing the large waste bags that had been brought especially for them, and carried into the storage space in the car park. And there they rest to this very day as a pleasant reminder: every time the bags make it difficult for her to extract her bike, she remembers the way things worked out that day and the next and she feels glad—all's well that ends well.

When the employer-woman reached the family's home that morning to pick up her worker, she was warmly welcomed. No one showed their fears—neither the worker nor his wife nor his older and younger children nor his old father, who had lived through the War of 1948 and had amazing stories to tell from those days, nor his old mother, resting in her usual armchair, her legs folded beneath her, her lined face all happy at the sight of her son and daughter-in-law and grandchildren around her all well and whole, still familiar and dear to her in the dusk of her mind.

After all the usual gestures of hospitality were performed, greetings and blessings and sweet juice and sweet mint tea and bitter black coffee, and she had eaten of the fruit of the vine and the fig tree and sat some more in the small living room while the TV screen flickered with scenes of other people's horrendous disasters—homes bombed with barrels of explosives in Syria and terrified people running hither and thither among the ruins—after spending a rather long time this way, she suggested that she and the father finally get on their way. And although only the two of them were intending to leave, everyone except the grandmother, whose feet no longer carried her, hurried to get up and out and stood around the red Ford Fiesta next to the house in the deserted street.

"How should we travel?" she asked the worker-father.

"In the trunk," he answered.

She had hoped he'd sit next to her, as they had often done when he still had his permit, although back then, too, they were not supposed to cross together at the same crossing: a Jew and an Arab-resident-of-the-Territories. But back then they could say they didn't know, and then turn back.

"Have you ever traveled this way before?" she asked.

"What does it matter?" he answered. Realizing she wasn't satisfied, he added with a smile: "One gets used to it, this is our life, and we want to live."

Literally.

They had already gotten used to many things together, he and she, things pleasant and less pleasant. He for his part, she for hers, since as has already been said, her part in no way resembles his. Even the ties between them as with several of the protagonists of the other stories told here, have known their ups and downs. At times this man really troubled her in his strong will to resist his life, his will to broaden the narrow horizon that limits it more and more and to extricate himself with her help from this unending distress. But she had not always been willing to help in the ways that he asked her, and two or three times she had broken her ties with him. How easy it was in the age of identified calls: she simply didn't answer. And he could not come to her home, after all. Perhaps this, too, is a reason for the existence of the Separation Barrier, to help those on this side not to help those on the other side. But their ties were always renewed—even anger and disappointment had become part of a true relationship.

Now he opened the empty trunk, sat inside it, lay down folded up on his side, and closed the red metal lid over himself. His wife and father smiled. He also closed over himself the inner black-padded cover and raised it back again right away: the window had to be opened, he didn't have enough air. She got in the car, fumbled with the key in a not very steady hand and stuck it in the ignition, turned it halfway and then pressed the button to open the back left window. He raised the black cover a few centimeters and said that would do, and lowered it again. The woman seated at the wheel looked at the empty black seat next to her, she looked at the rear-view mirror and saw the empty black seat behind her and the black emptiness behind it, and her belly contracted.

Suddenly she couldn't bear her loneliness. She looked out, taking in the relatives who still stood there smiling. Her eyes lingered on the hairstylist-student daughter, who gave her a mischievous look, or perhaps it only seemed so to her.

How young and pretty this girl was, she thought. What she herself needed now was for the girl to sit next to her, to come along with her, keep her company. She pressed the button, brought down the right-hand window, leaned over, and called out to the girl. "Come along," she urged, "come with us. After all, you have always asked me to smuggle you over to see Jerusalem for the first time ever."

Young and pretty and nimble. Five minutes and she was ready for the road—a nice overnight bag slung over her shoulder and her slim figure tucked tightly into a blouse and pants, with a matching little jacket adding just the right touch of chic. Her long black hair was loose, flowing down smooth and shiny over her shoulders and down her back, while her dark almond eyes were hidden by stylish sunglasses and aroused curiosity, and even a desire to discover what was behind them, the secret of this girl in the flower of youth, whether a secret was indeed there or not.

She got in the car and now, as her presence and the fragrance of her soap filled the empty space, the spirits of the woman at the wheel lifted. She turned on the ignition and got into driving gear, and all three travelers waved goodbye—the trunk cover was raised slightly for this purpose and a moving hand could be seen—and they got on their way. As she backed up the car she saw that even the grandmother was now sitting, legs crossed beneath her, on the small stoop, waving goodbye with a big smile.

Near the checkpoint, a rather long line of Israeli cars waited. Mostly, she knew, they contained settlers driving either to work or to run errands in Jerusalem. Thus the line proceeded quickly. And when their turn came, they too passed safely by the security guards and soldiers, who didn't pay attention to the two women sitting in front, upright and visible, let alone to the person folded up in back, out of sight. When they got to the other side and exhaled in relief, visibly and invisibly, a negotiation began. The stowaway wished to get out of the trunk, and the confused driver didn't know how to let him do this: she couldn't stop on this high-speed road. What, should she pull over and open the trunk and he would get out and straighten up and open the back door of the car to sit and ride as if nothing happened? Now she was really scared. He said something and she didn't quite hear it—she was hard of hearing. And perhaps she was now hard of understanding too, or didn't want to grasp what his daughter was explaining to her on his behalf—that there was no need for her to pull over, her father would get out of the trunk as she drove. The driver looked at the rear-view mirror and at the side mirrors, she looked at the cars moving behind her and said, startled: No, it's impossible here, people will see and tell. They should wait for some side road.

As they were negotiating, in her rear-view mirror she saw long thin fingers hugging the top of the backseat, leading a hand and a wrist and an arm, and in a moment a head and a body. The lean man crawled over the back of the seat, landed softly, and sat.

"Good morning, guys! *Sabah al kheir, ya jama'a!*" The voice of the third traveler in the back sounded almost merry, and his daughter answered right away: "Good morning, Dad! *Sabah al nur, ya baba!*"

The surprised driver grew silent, focused her gaze, and pricked up her ears. Then she grew calm: no car slowed down in front, no car honked behind. Meanwhile the voice of the man who was no longer willing to remain invisible resounded from the backseat and wished them a good morning again, his hand stroking his daughter's long hair as he joked and asked if a guy is not allowed to go to sleep in a car and wake up and sit up—it's allowed, isn't it? Well, there, he said, he had a good nap and now he was awake: *Salaam 'aleikum!*

She, the driver, will not forget the happy smiles of both her passengers that morning, nor her own smile. What a relief, what a good feeling now filled the car instead of the stress that was there just a little while ago. Now they sat there for all to see: a young woman and an older woman in front, and in the back a man in his best years, though no longer in the best of health—she knew this quite well, since the man does not spare her his tales of woe.

And so all three reached Jerusalem safe and sound, and the father told his daughter that she was now in Jerusalem, the Holy City, but the woman at the wheel did not go out of the way to show her around, nor did she slow down nor stop, but rather she drove directly to the empty apartment that needed a new coat of paint. When they entered, the house painter and plasterer and whitewasher, for whose sake and for the sake of whose livelihood this whole strange trip had been taken, checked out the walls and their flaws and said, just as she had feared he would, that it was a two-day job at least, if not three. He would sleep here overnight, of course, but what about his daughter—could she spend the night over at her place? She was a conscientious worker, she could help her cook, clean . . .

The employer/landlord could not believe her own ears: Cook? Clean? What, had she brought along an illegal alien housemaid as well? And another negotiation got under way: His daughter did not come here to work, the woman said angrily; they would drive around and she would show her Jerusalem. But one day was quite enough for the painting: the flat was small, and the ceilings didn't need painting. Nor did the kitchen.

"No, one day won't do," he insisted. "Look at all the holes in the walls."

"There aren't so many," she countered, "and they can be filled right away—even I know how to do that."

"The ceiling over there in the room has a wet stain, look, it needs to be scraped and then sanded and then plastered and then whitewashed. And the kitchen walls aren't that clean anymore. And why not paint the doors while we're at it?"

"All right," she gave in. "So a day and a half at most. Tomorrow afternoon we drive back."

"All right," he sighed, "I'll work twenty-four hours nonstop and get done. For you I'd do anything. You'll see—you'll be happy.

"Okay, a day and a half, and there's no need to work nonstop." Thus she concluded this unpleasant exchange.

She was never good at this familiar dialogue between a private employer and a workman. Especially not under these circumstances, when the dialogue was not just between an employer and a hired worker but also, and mainly, between a woman who lives in comfort and a man who spends all his days struggling, and under military occupation no less, for which she cannot help feeling responsible. They agreed, then, on a day and a half of work, rounded out to two days. And the daughter—sure, she could stay over at the woman's place. She would be her guest, and the woman would show her Jerusalem.

"What would you like to do—what do you want to see?" She turned to the daughter, having gotten used to the idea that they would stay together. And in fact this girl, whom she had known since her childhood and whom she had already taken to the beach once, was very likable and the woman was happy to have her over and give her a good time in Jerusalem. After all, this was exactly the kind of freedom she likes, the freedom she enjoys in this enslaving country, the freedom that had already become her philosophy of life and a source of joie de vivre.

The girl listed her wishes: (1) She'd like to ride a bike. (Really? The hostess was very surprised: all of her Palestinian friends and acquaintances know that she herself rides a bike, and she had no doubt that they see this as another one of her weird ways, but on the part of the girl this wish was rebellious, for women in conservative Muslim society are not supposed to ride a bike.) (2) She wishes to take a train ride. She has never ever been on a train, and Jerusalem does have one. (3) She would like to visit the Old City and perhaps even pray at the Al Aqsa Mosque.

These were her wishes, and in that order.

The father, naturally, was not going to take part in any of these outings; he said he wouldn't even step out of the apartment, for if he did he might get caught. He wouldn't even go out for cigarettes and refreshments (in other words, his employer needed to get him some right away), and anyway he had come here to work, not to have a good time. And there was plenty of work to be done! (He had already said this before in no uncertain terms!) But how would he work? Where's the paint and the buckets and the cement and the plaster and the scraper and the sandpaper and the ladder? There is nothing here. He ordered his employer, then, to write down everything he needed and to go out and shop for it and bring it. His daughter could help her carry it.

So that was how the two of them took their first trip in the Holy City: a shopping trek to the Mahane Yehuda market. They rode part of the way in the car. Then she parked the car at the outer edge of the market, and on their way to Agripas Street, where the shops were, she led her guest through some picturesque winding alleys. She was glad to show them to her; perhaps she even said to her invited-uninvited tourist—tourist?—that this neighborhood, Nachla'ot, is one of the first Jewish neighborhoods to be built outside the Old City walls. Yes, she's sure she told her that. But the young woman, who while they were in the car had not stopped bragging to her friends on the phone about the details of her adventure, and had even admitted to them that she was going about with her head uncovered, now walked beside her silently.

As they began to walk up Agripas Street, it was already clear to the hostess that neither she nor her companion was really enjoying herself. The sun was already scorching, and the buses that fill this narrow street at all hours of the day, bumper to bumper, flooded them with their noise, threatening to run them over as well as the rest of the people wending their way in between, carrying large shopping bags. That's what Agripas Street is like now: a loathsome trail of trials and tribulations. Since the main Jaffa Street was transformed into the light rail route, all bus traffic into the center of town has been diverted to Agripas, and this ancient street, handsome in its unique way, has been hopelessly ruined. Scandalous.

She wished to explain this to her silent guest, but the noise all around overcame her voice, and anyway she wasn't sure she should speak in Arabic around here, in this place where there is always graffiti with messages such as "Death to Arabs!" or "Don't buy from Arabs!" And the young guest—the hostess finally realized—had obviously already had enough of the sights and did not need explanations, certainly none about the quality of urban life.

At the hardware store she was provided with the items she had listed and was even offered help in getting them to her car: where was the car?

"The car isn't here," she said.

"What, you mean to carry all of this?" the storekeeper asked her.

"There are two of us," she said, "and we can do two rounds; the car isn't that far."

The storekeeper looked her over, and then the other woman: the one was getting on in years, and this one was slim and fragile—she read this in his face. No, they couldn't, he ruled. Go ahead, try to lift the fifteen-liter paint bucket. How did she imagine they could? It's a joke, ridiculous. —All right, so she'll go get the car. But where would she park here? —No need to park, the man said, no longer young but still very good-looking. She can stop on the sidewalk by the shop entrance and won't even have to get out of the car. He'll see this pretty young lady sitting next to her and will come running with all the stuff.

Really? The woman glanced apprehensively at the silent girl and couldn't keep from translating for her the compliment she had just received. Whether or not the storekeeper was listening, no one in the shop minded the unexpected language that was pronounced unsurely by the older woman. All eyes were on the younger one. Not one but three smiling faces now stared at her: the owner, one of his employees, and she herself, noticing once again how pretty her guest was. The young woman finally smiled. This was how Jerusalem served them their first moment of fun.

But when they returned with all the supplies—they even shopped for food and drink on the way—to the father who was waiting idly in the apartment, hungry and thirsty and dying for a smoke, the two were already exhausted from the heat and the errands, and probably also from the unspoken tension that had filled the beginning of this shared day. Now they just longed to rest, which was not possible at this point except in the privacy of the hostess's home.

They left the father, then, equipped for his day and a half of work, and hurried to drive on to the air-conditioned apartment in Beit Ha-Kerem. And indeed as soon as they crossed the threshold and closed the door behind them, they both felt relieved, especially the guest. The bike and the train and the Old City and the mosques were forgotten. She put her bag in the room that was assigned to her, showered, put on the pink flowery nightgown the hostess had provided, which suited her even though it was too large, went back into the living room, picked a book in Arabic from a bookshelf, and fell asleep over it on the sofa. She did not seek the quiet of a room of her own.

When she awoke, she paced the flat awhile, exploring it with curiosity and wonder, and went back to the living room, where her hostess was sitting trying to concentrate on the editing job she had to finish for a meeting later that day. After all, she hadn't known things would turn out the way they had. The guest promised the hostess that she would let her work and to that end accepted the suggestion to sit alone in the garden for a while before they proceeded together to the café where that work meeting was to take place.

On her way to the garden, still wearing the nightgown and barefoot, the guest chose another Arabic book from the bookshelf, sat down under the vine in the padded wicker chair, took a sip of the coffee that was served to her on the matching wicker table, put the book on her knees, opened it, and immediately placed her cell phone on it. Then she gave the hostess, who was still standing there to serve her, a merry look and called out happily, *Ma ahla!* How lovely! before inserting the earbuds that were connected to the cell phone and turning to her own entertainment world. The hostess fondly eyed her beloved garden, now blooming profusely, gave herself a satisfied inner pat on the back, and returned to the living room to do her work.

But after hardly any time at all the girl returned and sat down on the chair facing her with a winning smile, meaning: I've rested enough, and now let's go out. "Not yet, just a little more patience," the woman said. Another three pages and she will be done, and they'll go to the nice café on the Hebrew University campus, called the Hebrew Restaurant, where her work meeting will be held. They will walk around the green campus, she will show her the gym and the pool, and they will eat and drink at the restaurant. Her guest will have a nice and interesting time there.

Of course, I'll be patient, the young woman said sweetly. She got up to take yet another book in Arabic from the shelf and seated herself facing the woman, placing the book in her lap and looking at the hostess with her dark almond-shaped eyes, as if to say: I'm waiting here quietly, go on working . . . what, am I distracting you?"

Yes, she is distracting. What can I do, the seventy-one-year-old hostess sighed inwardly—their age difference is over fifty years, and there are other gaps besides.

She suggested the young woman get dressed and ready to go out—perhaps by then the woman would manage to finish her work. (Oh, she's just so diligent, this woman! Diligent and disciplined sometimes even to the point of being boring.) And the work did indeed get done, because the guest's preparations took a while this time. When she came back into the living room she was wearing a different blouse and jacket, even tighter than before, and her face was made up delicately and in good taste, and her long hair, which she had earlier put up in a loose bun for her nap, was now down over her shoulders, combed and smooth and shiny.

The young woman paused to examine herself in the mirror by the door before they left, but in the car she was apparently still not satisfied, for she turned the rear-view mirror toward herself and made a slight adjustment to the part in her hair. The driver turned the mirror back to its place; the passenger turned it toward herself again—just for a moment, she pleaded—and the driver scolded and the passenger apologized and stopped.

So that was how the two of them went out to spend their afternoon.


And whom did they meet at the restaurant? What a coincidence—the ophthalmologist! He was sitting with a woman friend at a table with coffee and pastries. She approached him and introduced the girl to him and told him what she had done, which he himself—that's what she told him—had pushed her to do. Here, this is the daughter of the worker she had smuggled this morning in the trunk of her car, as after that talk in the gym she had looked into it and discovered that both the authorities and the employers—whether real or fictitious—charge a fortune

for every single entry permit. Actually she had already told him
of the results of her inquiry over the phone, and he had thanked
her for taking the trouble, but now it was difficult to gauge
the expression on his face—astonishment? embarrassment? He
kept silent for a moment and then surprised her, saying: "You
know what? After we spoke I was thinking I might join you."

Join her how, join her by doing what? She did not ask
and he didn't specify. After they had been seated at their own
table and were having a good time, she and her guest and her
colleague—a young Israeli professor of Arabic literature who
spoke fluent Arabic and delighted the younger woman with
his conversation and his listening. The ophthalmologist approached them on his way out, held out his hand to the girl
with a gentlemanly bow wishing her, in Hebrew, a nice time in
Jerusalem, and hurried out. The woman called out after him:
"Remember, you said you'd join me!"

He turned back and replied, "I didn't say I would. I said I'm
considering it." And he went on his way.

After the older and younger woman walked around the campus and in the gym area, as promised, they went back home deciding to leave the rest of their planned outings for the next day.

The next day the bicycle issue was fortunately forgotten, but
they did ride the light rail. They got off at the Damascus Gate
stop, and there the hostess told the guest that if she wished she
could now cover her hair without fear, for here she was mostly
among Muslims. But the girl didn't want to, preferring to keep her
long hair loose. She looked around her, beaming and a bit defiant.

For hours they walked through Old City alleys and pilgrim-
filled churches, whose rituals and symbols the young woman
found very interesting, and then they entered a Christian hos-
pice whose roof offers a panoramic view of the city and the

Dome of the Rock and the Al Aqsa Mosque. The hostess noticed a large poster hanging on the front of the building announcing—in English and Arabic—a photography exhibition
from Gaza displayed inside, but the guest would not let her
linger in front of the sad photos but urged her to climb up to
the roof. There they looked together at the really marvelous
view, including the compound of the famous Haram A-Sharif
(Dome of the Rock), and took each other's picture. The guest
phoned her mother and father to tell them what she was seeing
and was beside herself with sheer excitement. "How wonderful
it all is," she told her hostess, "and I thank you so much, you
have made my dream come true." A dream and at its heart a
wall: they did not go to the Al Aqsa Mosque, for they had
a silent agreement—both of them were afraid.

They concluded their tour of East Jerusalem with a walk
along Salah A-Din Street outside the Old City, at the young
woman's request. There they passed many clothing shops, but
the hostess urged her guest to enter a bookstore instead. And
she bought her the excellent book *The Yacoubian Building* by
the Egyptian novelist 'Alaa Al-Aswani (which, of all the books
the young woman had removed from the hostess's Arabic literature bookshelf, she finally did begin to read before going
to sleep, and must have found interesting—it is a very juicy
book). And then they were exhausted again from the heat of
the sun and the marvels of their experiences—exhausted but
happy. Both of them were a bit dreamy as they sat together and
apart in the light rail on their way back to her apartment in the
western part of the city. Each with her own dreams.

In the late afternoon they picked up the father, who had
finished his work at the apartment to the full satisfaction of his
employer, and drove back to the village, seated for anyone to

see in the red Ford Fiesta, she and the older male illegal alien
and the younger female illegal alien, because the checkpoint in
that direction was usually open to all.


At home in the village all of the family members were gathered to welcome them, the grandmother in her armchair with
her legs folded beneath her and the grandfather sitting in his
armchair and still holding his stick, and the mother and the
daughters and the son, and again refreshments were served with
sweet juice and sweet mint tea and bitter black coffee and the
fruit of the vine and figs.

When the mother heard that her daughter had been to Salah
A-Din Street, she said she too had been there not too long
ago—she'd had an entry permit for a doctor's appointment.
What a wonderful street, what shops!

"Want to see what I bought for me and the girls at Salah
A-Din?" the mother asked, and without waiting for a reply
brought three dresses from another room and displayed them
one by one, listing their advantages and low prices.

"We bought a book on Salah A-Din," the daughter said and
took *The Yacoubian Building* out of her handbag and handed it
to her mother. The mother leafed through it a bit and placed
it on the sofa next to the dresses. The hostess, who was now a
guest, shifted uneasily in her seat and felt a little embarrassed:
perhaps buying that book was a mistake?

Was she cursed or blessed?

Blessed, clearly, for then the grandmother held out her ema-
ciated arm, inviting her to approach, and placed her hand on
the woman's head and blessed her with light in her eyes.

All's well that ends well.

# PRISONERS

And furthermore I saw under the sun a place of
judgment and wickedness was there . . .

*Ecclesiastes* 3:16

# The Story
# of Adnan Abdallah

The prison covering an area of 400,000 sq.m. is located in the Halutza
dunes of the north-western Negev desert near the Egyptian border. . . .
The outside appearance of the prison is that of a giant castle,
camouflage-painted in the midst of the desert. Its vast inner spaces
include huge tents whereas the built-up wings are surrounded
by watchtowers rising above the incarceration compounds.

FROM THE ISRAEL PRISON SERVICE'S WEBSITE,
National Prison Organization, Ketzi'ot Prison

On the whole the Castle, as it appeared from this distance, corresponded
to K.'s expectations. It was neither an old knight's fortress nor a
magnificent new edifice, but a large complex, made up of a few
two-story buildings and many lower, tightly packed ones; had one
not known that this was a castle, one could have taken it for a small
town. K. saw only one tower, whether it belonged to a dwelling or a
church was impossible to tell. Swarms of crows circled round it.

FRANZ KAFKA, *The Castle* (translated by Mark Harman)

## *A Tale of Eyeglasses*

The cab driver followed the blue-and-white sign standing alone
in the Halutza dunes of the Negev desert and turned left onto
a side road: it said Ketzi'ot Prison. The cab passed a rundown
roadside kiosk and an abandoned gas station; then the long
desert-colored concrete wall came into sight, crowned with

barbed wire, and the concrete towers rising above it, and the
cables stretching out from it and behind it in every direction
among the electricity poles and lamp posts and perhaps farther
on to other facilities too, out of sight even from close up: the
huge tents were not to be seen, nor the built-up wings and
certainly not the prisoners.

The driver continued a bit and then stopped by a barbed-
wire fence with a sign in Hebrew and Arabic fixed to it, welcoming those who come to the military court Ketzi'ot and
announcing that this was the attorneys' entrance. The entrance
itself was hidden behind a multitude of pallets bearing all sorts
of construction and roofing and coating materials, which despite their ugliness were clothed in the fresh green leaves of a
virile creeper that clung to them with its tendrils and climbed
toward the cascading galvanized roofs, one on top of the other,
and crawled and spread on and on, and bore its fresh green
tidings to places where the eye could no longer follow.

Behind that entrance, on that day, September 29, 2009, Adnan
Abdallah waited for his case to be reviewed. Two elderly women
stepped out of the cab and walked toward the entrance, one with
her walking stick and the other with her backpack, the first an
attorney who represented Adnan and the other Adnan's friend,
who exactly one year and two days earlier had written a personal
affidavit submitted to the military court. It read as follows:

*Personal testimony regarding Mr. Adnan Abdallah, ID no.*

———————

Your honor, the Military Judge,

I, the undersigned, a senior editor in the venerable Israeli
publishing house Am Oved, a translator and a writer, hereby

attest that I am well acquainted and befriended with Adnan Abdallah.

Since we became acquainted, and especially in recent months, we have had numerous talks about both political and personal matters. I am aware of the fact that Adnan is now held in administrative detention, and given this context I wish to note that in all of my conversations with him, on matters of culture and ideology as well as personal matters, Adnan has stood out as a gentle, warm and cordial person, a lover of people and of peace and endowed with enormous intellectual and cultural curiosity. Time and again he has expressed his hope for peace between our two peoples and in this matter he is the optimist of the two of us—at times even naive, in my opinion.

He has tried to convince me, much older than he and more skeptical, that a peaceful solution between two states is not at all unrealistic. Sometimes it seemed to me that he wanted this peace and a normal life for all of us so much— after he himself had already been imprisoned for quite a few years—that psychologically he is simply unable to stop believing in this possibility.

Consequently, as it seems to me, Adnan applied himself to the study of Israeli society in a course of sociology at Abu Dis University. He was very diligent in his work and aspired to excel. He told me in great detail about the lecturers and various course subjects, about his marks and the examinations he was about to take, and of his eventual plans to pursue postgraduate studies.

Not only were his mind and time dedicated exclusively to his studies, but he even told me in one of our talk, that the time he had already spent in prison was a steep enough price for his militancy and that from now on he had no intention of acting unlawfully, for most important for him at this point was to concentrate on his private life, study, and find professional work and a livelihood. He also remarked that his wife would not be able to cope with another forced separation from him due to his incarceration and was adamant that he avoid this at all costs.

There was no kind of a formal statement in this specific personal conversation: we simply spoke about our lives, his and mine. Therefore I believe he spoke with the spontaneity and sincerity that characterize him: a man who while holding political views and being publicly involved in his own society—he does not conceal any of this—still wishes to live his private life in spite of all the hardships he faces under the present circumstances.

In the spirit of openness and sincerity that characterize Adnan, I wish to attest here that I too am a citizen engaged both politically and publicly, situated on what is called the "left wing" of the political spectrum. Even so I would rather define myself first and foremost as an Israeli Jewish woman with humanist values, moved to defend them actively in my own country, where I was born and to which I am profoundly attached. This is how my parents raised me, especially my mother, whose family members were murdered by the Nazis, and she herself experienced two world wars and was not fortunate enough to witness the peace for which she was active right up to a very advanced age. Her dream was shattered, and I wish to continue being active to achieve it.

In Adnan I have found an interlocutor who shares my belief in these values. I seek such partners on the other side of the political and inhumane barrier that has been erected between the two peoples here because of the conflict. In consideration of all of the above, I ask the military court to be attentive to this voice of mine as well when it comes to ruling on the continued denial of Adnan Abdallah's freedom: please give it back to him—even in dispute he is our interlocutor, not our enemy.

Dr. Ilana Hammerman,
Jerusalem, September 27, 2008

The affidavit did no good, apparently, as one year and two days had gone by since it was written, and Adnan was still being held in administrative detention. During this time an extraordinary tale of eyeglasses had unfolded.

Here is the tale.

Adnan is nearsighted, and his eyeglasses were broken during his incarceration. The website of the national prison organization stipulated at that time—perhaps it still does—that "the facility contains a medical staff of physicians, dentists and paramedics who provide prisoners with medical care," but perhaps this medical staff did not include an optometrist, or perhaps the optometrist was not available soon enough to determine what eyeglasses Adnan needed, and therefore Adnan turned to that woman who, as declared in the quoted document, was his friend.

"I think I need 2 or perhaps 2.5 diopter lenses," he urged during a prohibited phone call from Ketzi'ot Prison. "I'm having a hard time without glasses."

She, a glasses wearer herself since her long-gone early youth, understood him and hurried out to the excellent old optometrist's shop in Jerusalem where she is a regular customer.

"Well, what's your advice, 2 or 2.5?" she asked the owner, an experienced optometrist.

"How can I tell? The gentleman has to come in himself," he answered.

"The gentleman is in prison," she told him.

The optometrist was very surprised and fell silent for a moment. "Sorry, I can't advise you; it would be unprofessional," he ruled.

The woman deliberated briefly. "Well then, we have to take a chance: 2.5," she said.

"All right. And what about astigmatism—should it be a cylinder lens? Does he have astigmatism?" he asked her.

The woman decided immediately: "No, it's 2.5 diopters, that's it," she told him.

Now she had to choose a frame.

"Please help me choose a frame," she asked him. "A fashionable frame for a thirty-five-year old man."

They went over to the white cases lining the walls of the shop, and she looked on as shallow drawers were pulled out one by one. Each drawer and its frames: horn-rimmed and metal, round and square, small and medium and large frames, and rimless glasses with only a thin nose bridge and very thin arms for the ears. And to every frame a tiny white price tag was tied with a bit of string: 199 shekels, 399 shekels, 999 shekels, 1,499 shekels . . .

The woman couldn't make up her mind.

Finally for Adnan's round-squarish face she chose a metal frame that was somewhat round and somewhat squarish at 459 shekels, with scratch-free-coated lenses. Two days went by and the glasses were ready. They were presented to her on the counter and then inserted in a hard black case with a soft burgundy-colored cleaning cloth. The woman was happy with her choice and with the case as well, which seemed appropriate to protect the glasses on their long journey to the Halutza dunes and during their prison time among those dunes. She then applied in writing to the Prison Service for permission to visit Adnan in order to deliver his glasses. The reply came soon enough. It contained three items:

1. Your request has been examined by the authorities at Ketzi'ot Prison. Note that an administrative detainee is allowed to receive only family visits.
2. In view of the above and after consulting the relevant authorities, it has been ruled not to allow the prisoner a visit by a non-family member.
3. For your information.

The woman found this formulation somewhat awkward, but still the refusal was clear and final. This being the case, she had to find another way of getting the glasses to Adnan.

She found out that orders of administrative detention were subject to periodic "judicial reviews." They are presided over by a military judge and allow the detainee to be represented by an attorney. She found out further that such a review of Adnan's case was scheduled very soon at the military court in Ketzi'ot, which in this case was referred to as the Military Court for Administrative Affairs, and his attorney was about to travel there in order to represent her client. The woman asked the attorney to pass the glasses on to Adnan.

To this end all she had to do was send the glasses to the attorney's Tel Aviv home, and so she did. She even went out of her way: as the matter was urgent she sent the glasses by special delivery, packed in a padded envelope. But when she called the attorney late that afternoon she heard to her surprise and dismay that the package had not arrived. She called the Israel Post and the Israel Post directed her to the special-delivery customer services. The special-delivery clerk checked and found that the addressee had not been home nor answered her phone and therefore was not available to receive delivery of the package. The annoyed sender suggested that the addressee was hard of hearing and perhaps did not hear the doorbell ring nor the slightly longer telephone ring. But the clerk did not know what to say to that, and the woman now had no other choice but to note down some telephone numbers in order to pursue her inquiry and take care of the matter. One of the numbers, a woman's voice later informed her over the phone, was the reception at "Tel Aviv Granaries."

Still, two days later the envelope was handed to the attorney, and on the next day both arrived at the prison in the Halutza dunes.

However, the glasses themselves did not reach Adnan's nose that day, for it turned out that in order to get there certain procedures were required: the prisoner was supposed to have submitted a special written request to the prison warden, the warden would then look into the request, decide whether to agree or not, and inform the lower echelons of his decision. And here, in this case, such procedures had not been undertaken. Or perhaps they were already started but were still under way. In any event, the attorney was not allowed to bring the glasses into the military court compound.

She returned to Tel Aviv with the glasses.


Days, weeks, maybe even months went by, and the attorney who had appealed against Adnan's detention was summoned to a session at the military court in Ketzi'ot, which in this case was referred to as the Administrative Detentions Military Appellate Court. She drove there, and the glasses traveled with her again.

This time she was allowed to bring the glasses into the military court compound, and they even crossed the threshold of the hall where the review of the appeal of detention was to be held. The attorney placed the eyeglass case on the table that was allotted her, and Adnan gave it a yearning nearsighted look. The attorney asked permission to hand it to him, put it in his hands that were held out to her, but the Prison Service guards said: No, impossible, it's prohibited! Because although the special request had been submitted to the warden, a reply had not yet been provided, either affirmative or negative.

The military judge intervened and recommended that the glasses be given to Adnan. "Why not?" he asked. "Why can't the detainee's wishes be met on such a minor matter even if it is an exception to the strict letter of the law? After all, the detainee needs glasses." But all the attempts at persuasion made by the senior army officer who acted as judge in this court and really tried his best regarding the glasses, were no match for the "no" of the Prison Service men sitting in that hall: "No, your honor, impossible! These are the regulations!" End of the matter.

From this minor interaction one may learn something about the factors governing the military judicial and penitentiary system—of which one of the essential components is administrative detention without indictment, trial, or verdict. A lesson learned even before one goes through the records of the hearings of Adnan's case—as the woman who had bought his glasses did later in order to understand from more important and essential details the absurdity of this tragicomic spectacle which this system produces incessantly in a multitude of variations.

In Adnan's case, however, this minor detail sufficed to generate a subplot that ended badly. Here it is.

Adnan—usually very restrained—lost it that day. He got on his feet at the defendants' dock, waved his arms, said he demanded to receive the glasses immediately, that he could not do without them, and would not calm down but rather got increasingly agitated and protested and yelled and spoke bluntly against his persecutors and even compared them to the persecutors of Jews in dark regimes of the past, which certainly was not appreciated by his guards. When the session was over—this the woman heard from the attorney the same day—he was taken straight to solitary confinement as punishment for his courtroom tantrum. Solitary—this the woman heard later from Adnan himself—was a filthy, cold cell, and the four days he spent locked up there were extremely bad days for him.

At any rate, that day the attorney returned to Tel Aviv with the glasses once more.


Since the appeal against administrative detention was rejected and the incarceration of administrative detainee Adnan Abdallah was extended for another six months, no court session was scheduled for the near future, and the woman who had bought him the glasses drove to the attorney's home to pick them up and take them back to Jerusalem. Now she thought of giving them to Adnan's family members, living in Deheishe refugee camp in the Bethlehem district, so that a family member allowed to visit would eventually take them to Adnan.

And sure enough, not long thereafter, Adnan was allowed a family-member visit. But none of the family members held an entry permit into Jerusalem, and the woman who brought the glasses was not allowed to enter the Deheishe refugee camp. She did have the privilege of being able to disregard this restriction rather easily without getting caught, and she had indeed done so occasionally, but since the matter of the glasses was too important and urgent to complicate and delay by disregarding the laws ruling these parts, she had the fortunate idea of changing the second part of her weekly bike trek and taking the glasses to the Beit Jala Junction on Road 60, where both Adnan's family and she herself were allowed.

It was a sunny, pleasant winter Saturday. The glasses inside their case were packed in her small backpack and rode with her across gorgeous landscapes, among wooded hills abloom with myriad winter flowers, up toward Bar-Giora, down to Beit Shemesh, and up to Tzur Hadassah. From there she intended to climb Road 375, pass by the ultra-Orthodox settlement of Beitar Ilit and the Palestinian village of Hussan, and freewheel down Road 60 to the Bethlehem area, totally hidden behind what is called the Separation Barrier, and which at that spot has been fancied up with a friendly facade of light-colored decorative stone. However, by the time she reached Tzur Hadassah the sky had clouded over, a cold drizzle had begun, and fog already filled the world around her along the horizon from one end to the other. Gone were the red tiled roofs of greening Tzur Hadassah, gone was the red sign that warned:

*Dear citizens!!! For fear that you might mistakenly and unwillingly enter the territory of the Palestinian Authority out of bounds for Israelis, the checkpoint soldiers have noted down your name address and ID as well as your license plate number. . . . Wishing you a good and safe journey, the IDF HQ in Judea and Samaria.*

Even the checkpoint itself disappeared, to the extent that the domains were totally blurred. And where was that large stone plaque welcoming travelers to the Jewish town of Torah and piety in the Judean Hills? And where was the village of Hussan facing that town of Torah? In fact, no plaque welcomes those who wish to enter its alleys, houses, and mosques, and its name has even been cut out of the green road sign that on other days is quite visible on the side of the road. But had it not been for the fog, its houses and minarcts would have emerged behind the tall barbed-wire fence—perhaps three times the height of an average human adult—erected against the stones occasionally hurled from there at cars driving along this road. Now even the fence was not visible—no checkpoint nor signs nor houses nor mosques nor even a barbed-wire fence! This entire flawed and conflicted and hostile piece of land was swallowed up by the fog. Alarmed, the cyclist turned to get back to Jerusalem as quickly as she could. She got home wet but in one piece and the glasses were still with her; they too were in one piece and even dry inside their case, together with the soft burgundy-colored cleaning cloth tucked in with them.

The family member went to visit Adnan without them.


Several more weeks passed, and the glasses were handed to friends of Adnan who had an entry permit into Jerusalem and came to her home to collect them. The friends gave them to his family members, and the next one who traveled to visit Adnan in prison took them with him. However, he too was not allowed to give them to him, the requested special permission had not yet been granted, and he too came back with them.

The man who took them and finally came back without

them was just an acquaintance of Adnan's from Deheishe, a relative of another prisoner in the camp, and he did get permission to place the glasses in the hands of the Ketzi'ot guards, who in turn gave them to Adnan. As simple as that. End of the tale of the eyeglasses.

## The Bird Fable

In the meantime lo, the winter is past, the rain is over and gone, and spring came, and summer came and was almost over, and bespectacled Adnan was still imprisoned at Ketzi'ot. Now he could see and read comfortably, however, and what's more, his prison conditions had improved: from the tent where for many months he had lived crowded with another twenty prisoners—freezing on winter nights and "boiling like a kettle" in the summer—he was transferred to a barrack to be imprisoned with only seven other inmates.

"And every two share an electric fan, just imagine!"

"Still you look rather ashen," she told him.

"Because I had a bad flu. Almost two weeks!" he said.

Those were the days of swine-flu panic.

Right away the woman moved her mouth away from the little round hearing holes in the transparent partition that separated them.

"Swine flu?"

"No," he laughed, "inmate flu. I'm perfectly all right now, don't worry."

She moved closer to the partition again and flattened her hand on it to meet his hand flattened toward her on the other side. A handshake of sorts.

He described his daily routine to her: rise at 6:30, exercise until 8:00, then breakfast, then reading or getting together for group studies, lunch, supper, bedtime. Three inmate counts a day: two short ones, ten by ten, one a bit longer, roll call— yes, names, not numbers. By this time inmates were no longer called by numbers as before, on account of the nasty comparisons that good souls and people of good taste had drawn with previous dark regimes.

"Good conditions," she said to him. "Sounds almost like a health resort, just as some people write in our press."

"No," he answered her, and produced a fable: "Take a bird from this arid desert and offer it life among the branches in the cool mountain woods around Jerusalem. Do you suppose it would want this?"

Adnan likes to quote fables and ask riddles from legends and children's stories.

"No, it wouldn't, it would want to live in its natural habitat, with its bird friends," he answered immediately, and offered the moral as well: "And so do I—I want to get back to my own surroundings."

He quit his fable talk and continued angrily: "Enough! I want to go home, home, I want to be free. Enough is enough! I can't stand prisons any longer! Or at least put me on trial and I'll know what I'm being held prisoner for and how long I'll be sitting here. The worst of it is thinking that I might be stuck here forever."

They sat facing each other in a room in the military court compound at Ketzi'ot, on both sides of that transparent partition. The room was intended for prisoners' meetings with their attorneys, and today was that September 29, 2009, on which, as has already been mentioned, the purchaser of the glasses came to the compound in the middle of the desert along with Adnan's attorney. The attorney had wrapped up her talk with her client and exited the room, and the other woman had come in unhindered and sat down facing the prisoner. She gave the glasses on his nose a satisfied look and recalled their winter journeys to and fro. But soon it will be winter again, she remarked sadly to herself—thirteen months and the fellow is still here! Thirteen months had passed in the following manner.

First came the administrative detention order signed by an officer of the Israel Defense Forces, worded as follows:

> By virtue of my authority stipulated in clause 1 of the edict regarding administrative detention (temporary orders) (Judea and Samaria) (number 1226), 1988, after examining the confidential data on the person named below and since to my understanding the matter is highly relevant to crucial security issues of the region and to public security, I hereby order the detention of Adnan Abdallah from _____ until _____ on the grounds of his activity in the military wing of the Popular Front for the Liberation of Palestine that jeopardizes the security of the region and the public.

Then came incarceration at Ketzi'ot Prison in the Halutza dunes.

And then his administrative detention was extended for six months by the following order:

> By virtue of my authority stipulated in clause 1(b) of the edict regarding administrative detention (temporary orders) [combined version] (Judea and Samaria) (number 1591), 2007, after examining the confidential security data on the person named below and since to my understanding the

matter is still highly relevant to crucial security issues, and
since I have reasonable grounds to assume that the security
of the region and of the public still requires these measures,
I hereby order the extension of detention of Adnan Abdallah
from _____ until _____ for his activity in the military
wing of the Popular Front for the Liberation of Palestine that
jeopardizes the security of the region and the public.

Then came the appeal against the extension of the administrative detention, and it was rejected. And then administrative
detention was extended a second time. And then came the appeal against the extension of the administrative detention for
the second time.

The woman who had bought Adnan's glasses told his attorney that she wished to testify as a witness for the defense
at the appeal of the second extension of his administrative detention. The attorney thought this might help and therefore
turned to the appropriate authorities, asking them to summon
her as a character witness for the defense. The woman was already known to them through the affidavit she had written on
Adnan's behalf.

This request resulted in several written documents: the defense made the request, the prosecution objected, and a certain military judge overruled the objection. This might have
indicated that he agreed to grant the defense's request, but the
military judge also wrote that he would allow the prosecution
to restate its objection. The prosecution took this opportunity
and restated its position in an additional document. However,
another military judge ruled to summon the witness for the
defense and allowed the prosecution to raise its objection at the
beginning of the hearing. And yet another military judge, se-

nior in rank to his two predecessors, finally granted the request, and the defense issued an official summons to the character witness for the defense. The defense requested that the Prison Service issue her a permit to enter the premises of the military court; the Prison Service acquiesced and issued a one-off entry permit.

And thus on September 29, 2009, the woman who had bought Adnan his glasses arrived at the gates of the castlelike prison in the Halutza dunes—which at the time, according to the national incarceration agency website, held about 2,200 security prisoners, all of them kept out of sight, they and the facilities that held them—and she entered and was inspected at the inspection posts and was allowed to continue into the premises and did so and found herself in a tidy courtyard, calm and pleasant inside its numerous fences, and a few men were present.

Prison guards and a few policemen were sitting at a simple rectangular table, speaking in hushed voices. Beyond the table stood four very small white pavilions, each of them with a closed metal door and a small barred window. When one of the iron doors opened from time to time and a prisoner came out of it, hands and feet shackled, even then the calm reigning in this place was not disturbed, for the shackled prisoner, accompanied by a guard, walked with ease—the chain on his ankles was long enough—and was quietly swallowed into the courtroom, situated at the edge of the courtyard.

Despite the fact that nearly all material regarding the prisoners on trial is classified—material that is therefore not discussed in court but seen only by the judge—the hearings in this courtroom are held "behind closed doors," no public allowed to attend, and thus the room stays very quiet. Without an audience there is no apparent need to close the doors, and they stayed open the day the woman was summoned as a witness. In any case, that courtroom didn't have "doors," merely a single common door that opened wide onto the small courtyard, and the dry, pleasant late-summer desert air and the chirping of free birds.

The birds chirped, and accompanied by their sound the woman came out of the small room where she had sat facing Adnan behind the transparent partition, and stood in the yard. Adnan himself exited from another door and joined her—on his own, unescorted by either warden or guard. The birds chirped, and accompanied by their song the long-legged woman and the shackled Adnan walked over to the open courtroom. Their steps were unhurried, even delicate. It was not because of the chain that they walked thus—for it was a long chain—but because no one urged them on. And no partition now separated them from each other, so the two were now practically strolling together in a leisurely manner, quite content.

The woman's testimony too was given in a calm, almost intimate, atmosphere with everybody listening close by: Adnan, who sat right near her behind the modest balustrade, the senior officer who acted as judge, an exceptionally gracious man who time and again asked the witness to slow down for the sake of the court's recorder, as well as the major who served as prosecutor, a gentle-looking man, slim and of light hair and complexion. To them and to the defense, the woman briefly summarized the story of Adnan's life:

He was born and raised in Deheishe refugee camp. At the age of fifteen he was very seriously wounded by soldiers firing on a local demonstration against the fence that enclosed the entire camp at the time. At the age of sixteen he joined various activities against the Israeli army and was arrested several times. His prison time now amounted to eleven of the thirty-five years of his life.

The woman told them that she had made Adnan's acquaintance after he was freed from his immediately prior incarceration, of five years, and that she met him and spoke with him often during the single year he spent as a free man—a year in which he decided that he had sacrificed quite enough of his physical and mental energies for the sake of his people's national struggle, and now, she tried to emphasize, he wished to complete his university studies and live his life with his wife, who had also had enough of their forced separations. Then she told them what she had already written and submitted over a year earlier, that from her extensive political and personal talks with him she was impressed with his sincerity and frankness, and that she therefore believed what he told her, that not merely for personal reasons but also for reasons of principle, he now upheld nonviolent struggle, for he believed—unlike her—that there was a good chance for peace between the two peoples and that armed struggle would not do.

As for Adnan's past deeds, for some of which he had stood trial and been convicted and served his full sentence—deeds that in the words of the verdict included handling weapons, although these did not actually harm anyone, and for which there were difficulties with the evidence," as the judge himself stated in that trial—she said, probably lowering her voice a bit, she did not know what she herself would have done in his place if she had been compelled to live under military occupation since the day she was born.

Once she concluded her testimony, she was required to

exit the courtroom due to the confidentiality of the session. She therefore had to find out later from reading the records—which she keeps to this day—what ensued. She learned that the judge who had treated her so graciously did not particularly consider what she said. He ruled that her words "did not carry sufficient weight of evidence as to the activities of the detainee. There is no doubt that the detainee's past deeds were not known to the witness beyond what she had seen and heard. His activity, exposed in the confidential material submitted to the court, is by definition confidential and therefore the witness could not possibly have been exposed to it."

Indeed she could not have been exposed to information regarding that activity—reports of rather dubious credibility, as will briefly be clarified below—and neither could the defense attorney or the defendant, nor anyone else outside the military system.

The order to extend Adnan's administrative detention was then reissued, although the judge himself ruled that the information ascribing to the detainee "current military activity . . . is not highly credible" and should therefore be ignored, and he therefore reduced the extension to three months instead of the default six-month term.

Still he ruled that this reduction was "not essential."

"Not essential? What does that mean?" the woman asked the attorney. She had been speaking with Adnan on the telephone from time to time—he would call her although it was forbidden, and to do so he would stand in line for the mobile phone purchased at an exorbitant price which someone had apparently pocketed, and that one device served numerous prisoners—and therefore she knew that whenever a six-month detention approached its termination date, Adnan would count the days, perhaps even the hours and minutes, hoping that this time he would finally be freed. So how the hell could a reduction of the term to three months be considered "not essential"?

"A nonessential reduction," the attorney explained to her, "means detention may be extended again. An essential reduction means that at the end of the stipulated period, the detainee is set free."

But in the meantime the prosecution already hurried to appeal the three-month reduction of Adnan's detention, even if "nonessential," because the material regarding his case—so it claimed—showed that his being out of prison soon "would irreversibly jeopardize the security of the region."


Sic: irreversibly!

Truth be told, the woman wished to delineate something entirely different to the military men from the testimony she had given in the contemptible legal circumstances under which Adnan's fate was discussed. She especially wanted to tell them something about what they consider "jeopardy":

"Perhaps you will listen to my voice for once, the voice of a woman who has lived here all her life, from war to war and in the bad days between the wars, and who is no less attached to this place than you are. I too am a member of this public which you have undertaken to defend and protect, and ensure its security, as the cliché goes that appears in all of your documents. And I argue against you that for many years now *you* are the ones who jeopardize me. Confining thousands of people behind fences and walls of towns and villages and prisons hidden away on the outskirts of cities and in the desert is not defense but rather a constant fanning of the flames that are bound to leap up time and again. I argue against you that Adnan in prison and desperate is far more dangerous to me than Adnan free. That the free Adnan is to me, and could also be to my compatriots and to you too, an interlocutor and not an enemy."

Less than two months later, even prior to the end date of the three-month "nonessential" extension, Adnan was suddenly freed. Since then he has completed his undergraduate and graduate studies, and is now working and living in Ramallah with his wife and the three children born to them.

# The Story of Jamil

## *The Visit*

The child threw up. Now of all times—after they had finally arrived and after her brother flashed her his fetching smile from behind a transparent partition, the smile of a twenty-year-old who wants to be a man and still looks like a boy—now of all times she threw up. She threw up and cried. And soiled the nice clothes she had worn for the trip, and soiled the floor too.

Her mother was already seated at the partition with her eyes fixed worriedly on the face of her son, to see whether his cheeks were still as full and brown as before, or perhaps they'd become drawn and pale, God forbid, and held the telephone receiver close to catch the tone of his voice and search for some hint of his mood. With her free hand she pushed her daughter away. And then one of those in charge produced a mop and demanded that she clean up.

No, she isn't cleaning anything up, she's come to see her son, the father will clean, she said, almost yelling at her husband, who stood there embarrassed and confused. He was not used to his wife yelling at him, nor was he any good at caring for vomiting children and certainly not at cleaning floors. In their family it's the job of the wife—she is all glorious within. But the wife, her whole attention, her feelings, her sensations, her entire body tense from anticipation through long days and nights, was focused on the son across the partition, the son she could not touch and had to use the phone to exchange words with. He had one receiver and they had two, one for the father and one for the mother. But only one of them could listen to him at a time, not both of them. This was no conference call. But there isn't that much to say under such circumstances anyway, in this large hall with dozens of people seated in long lines on both sides of a transparent partition and speaking into telephone receivers.

How are you?

All right.

How are things?

All right.

Are you eating?

Yes.

Food okay?

Yes. Not really.

What are they feeding you here?

Okay. No more food talk. Did you bring me the clothes I asked for? I'm too hot here.

Yes, I did. But they wouldn't let me bring them in.

Why not?

I brought you shorts, but they said that on the form you had filled out you asked for trousers. I brought sandals. But sandals are not allowed. I brought a green shirt, but green is forbidden, and so are light blue and navy blue. Give them a new list.

But I need sandals, I'm too hot in shoes.

What can we do? Sandals are forbidden . . .

The floor was now mopped clean—the father did it. Now he too was asking how are things and what's new and what's up. The girl still hadn't uttered a word. She was swallowing some last sobbing hiccups and waiting for this whole ordeal to be over so they could go home. And only yesterday she had been so happy to be allowed to visit her brother! What a disappointment, what shame! At home she'll shower, wash her hair, change her clothes, and be that mischievous nine-year-old again, capricious, coquettish, driving everyone around her crazy with her whimsical airs and graces: one moment she's a sweet child and the next she's nearly a seductive young woman—and now annoying, bothersome, a nuisance.

In order to visit the son jailed at Ofer military prison, north of Jerusalem, they had left their village, south of Jerusalem, at 4:00 a.m. The direct route from the village to the prison camp goes through Jerusalem, which they are not allowed to enter, so they had had to take a taxi to Bethlehem and from there a bus on a long roundabout route. They traveled for about an hour and a half and then got in line with the other visitors in front of an iron gate and waited for their name to be called. The rising sun began to warm up the chilly morning in the Jerusalem hills for an hour, two hours, but after three or four hours it was already searing as it beat down on their heads from the vast blue expanse of sky stretched over the hills, and the detention camp surrounded by concrete walls and barbed-wire fences—and the family's name had still not been called. Many who had arrived on later buses had already been summoned to pass through the gate—and this gate is but the first gate on the way to the transparent partition. They were still standing in front of it, waiting and waiting. And they had arrived so early.

Something went wrong here, didn't it? Even those in charge

there seemed to think so and agreed to check the documents that the father was holding: May 27, it said. Yes, today is May 27, they agreed. But your visit was supposed to be on the 24th—no visit for you today.

For three months now the mother's eyes had brimmed with quiet tears every time anyone mentioned her jailed son. She had gotten angry each time she was told that in this day and age any young man of her people worthy of the name does jail time, and perhaps her son would even be regarded as a hero when he got out. She answered that she needed no hero: if at least he had struggled, fought the occupier—but he hadn't, it was the last thing on his mind. So no, she wanted him home, at her side! In this strong mother, who had already known greater troubles, her daughter's incurable illness for instance, something had begun to fall apart irremediably in the past three months. And now she burst into a fit of weeping: no, she was not moving from here until she saw her child.

All right, go in: the powers that be acquiesced.

On the other side someone pressed an electric buzzer, and the narrow turnstile turned as the parents and the girl squeezed between its bars and continued through the gate. They then boarded a bus that delivered them to the next gate.

There they passed through another turnstile and looked around them and saw that they were inside a large courtyard where many of those who had preceded them were still waiting, some seated on the few plastic chairs placed for their convenience and most sitting on the concrete floor, out in the open, exposed to the elements on this very hot day. No trace of this morning's coolness. This courtyard did have toilets for their convenience. The last people leaving here would be given rags and mops and cleaning material and ordered to clean up those restrooms. This

family would be among those last ones to leave. In the meantime, occasionally a few names were announced. Those whose
names were called out lined up and passed through another gate
one by one and through another turnstile and vanished. But
the family name of the three of them was not called out here
either.

The father went to inquire. The mother dragged behind.

"Your visit was scheduled for May 24. Why didn't you
come?" they were told again. "Your son waited for you and no
one came," they were scolded.

But the paper they were holding said May 27!

"That's right. Too bad, but there's nothing to be done."

The father had already decided they were going back. The
mother, who usually had no say on such matters, was resolute
not to go back: if she was not allowed to see her son, only her
dead body would be dragged out of here.

Really embarrassing. Even for the people in charge of the
service, the Prison Service.

So what's to be done? Ignore them? Chase them away?

God forbid! What, have they no feelings, the people in
charge of service and order?

They did their best, they summoned someone in charge, and
then another and another, and finally the chief warden himself.
His heart, beating behind the uniform and the bulletproof vest,
was not made of stone either. He promised the woman, over-
whelmed with anger and despair, to arrange something.

He promised and was true to his word: he went to the
trouble of finding out that another prisoner's guests had not
arrived. They were scheduled for a visit on the 27th and so far
they were not there. Perhaps their papers showed the 30th. All
right then, the family could enter in their stead.

And they did.

And then, right in front of the transparent partition, the child threw up.

And the mother and the father sat there holding the receivers and trying to smile in spite of it all. Forty-five minutes exactly. For at the end of the forty-five minutes all the phones went dead with a remote press of an invisible button. And they got up with all the other visitors and left.

Again they passed through all the turnstiles and gates and fences and boarded the two buses again and rode a long while along the winding route they had taken on their way there and took a taxi once again.

At 5:00 p.m. they were back home. Thirteen hours for forty-five minutes. They won't take the girl with them next time, they said.

## Open Up! Army!

The story begins in the middle of the night of February 17, 2009. It was a cold and rainy night, one of the rainiest in a winter when most days and nights had been dry. At 2:00 a.m. loud banging was heard on the door of Jamil's family home, and eight family members, old and young alike, were startled out of their sleep: Open up! Army! Soldiers of the Israel Defense Forces entered the house. They came to take Jamil away.

And they took him.

No questions were answered, and arguments, entreaties, shouts, and sobs were to no avail. The mother, who for some moments blocked the soldiers with her body, managed to give him a chance to get dressed in his room and cover himself with the coat she threw at him, and he was restrained with plastic cuffs and taken outside. He left behind an empty bed and a mother and a father and four sisters and one brother, all dazed.

Later, along with other youngsters whose families had also been startled out of their sleep and taken out of their beds and homes, he waited for a long time on the main street of the village, blindfolded, hands shackled to a fence behind his back, with the rain falling on him and the others all blocked and shackled as he was. Thus they stood until all those whose names appeared on the soldiers' list were assembled. And then people watching from the roof of a neighboring house saw them vanish with their captors into military vehicles, and then saw the vehicles vanish with their prey.

For the first two days after Jamil's arrest no one could inform his parents of his whereabouts. On the third day, through the Red Cross they found out that he was being held in custody at the Etzyon Bloc police station, not far from their village, but it was impossible either to visit him or to appoint an attorney for him. On the eighth day they learned that he was at the Ofer military prison, where his little sister was to throw up some months later.

A visit was still impossible, but one could already read his bill of indictment.

It read as follows.

*This person is hereby accused of committing the following violations:*

*First count:*

*The violation:* membership of an illegal organization, violating clauses no. 84 and 85(1)(a) of the 1945 Defense (Emergency) Regulations

*Details:* the said accused, from 2006 or thereabouts until the date of his arrest, was a member or acted as a member of an illegal organization, in the region, namely:

During the said period of time, in Hussan, he was a member of the Popular Front for the Liberation of Palestine (PFLP), an illegal organization. As part of his activity the accused committed the following.

*Second count:*

*Violation:* attendance at an assembly of an illegal organization, a violation of regulation 85(1)(d) of the 1945 Defense (Emergency) Regulations.

*Details:* the said accused, in the region at the time specified in the first count, attended a meeting of an illegal organization, namely: on the said date, in the region, as part of his membership in the PFLP, he participated in parades celebrating the organization's founding.

*Third count:*

*Violation:* the said accused, in the region, at the time specified in the first count, carried out some work or performed some service for an illegal organization, namely: at the said date, in the region, as member of the PFLP, the accused together with other cell members wrote slogans for the organization.

Jamil denied having committed any of the violations ascribed to him in the bill of indictment.

## *Alibi*

If requested, the woman now writing the story of Jamil could have given him a solid and documented alibi for one whole day in the period of time during which most of the violations listed in his bill of indictment had supposedly occurred: "Between 2006 or thereabouts until the date of his arrest."

The photographs from that one day bear the date: November 30, 2008. On that dramatic day, marking the beginning of another long hard patch in the life of the defendant's family, the defendant was not present at any assembly of any illegal organization, nor did he take part in parades celebrating the founding of such an organization, nor did he write slogans for such an organization.

On that day he traveled with his parents and ill sister—not the little nine-year old girl who threw up in front of the telephone-receiver-equipped transparent partition, but his seventeen-year old sister—to Beilinson Hospital at the Rabin Medical Center in Petah Tiqwa, Israel.

The senior doctor who met them there for consultation told them that no cure was possible for the girl's grave illness except perhaps a difficult and risky operation: a kidney and a liver lobe transplant whose success was highly doubtful. He told them, further, that since the Israeli healthcare system does not provide organs for transplant to persons other than Israeli citizens, the girl's close relations would have to be examined and two compatible persons identified as donors. He said that the cost of such complex surgery would amount to about one million shekels. The doctor hoped that Jamil would prove to be a suitable donor as, unlike the parents, he was still young.

Although no indictment was involved here, of course this

too was a sort of verdict, more fateful, in fact. The actual sentence was not even conceivable at the time.

But this is not the place to tell the tale of the sick girl's life and how it was saved; rather this is a short episode of the life of her elder brother, a vigorous young man under no threat of death, either then nor later. Nor was he imprisoned yet inside the fences of a detention camp on November 30, 2008,—quite the opposite: on that bright autumn day he saw the sea for the first time in his life and had that sense of freedom that most people feel at the sight of the infinite expanse of water.

This is the story of Jamil's first encounter with the sea, a mere hour's drive from his home, a drive he is forbidden to take:

After hearing the senior doctor's harsh verdict, the woman who is presently writing the story of Jamil suggested that the four sad and tense family members spend some time at the Tel Aviv beach now that they were already with her in her red Ford Fiesta down from the hills and on the coastal plain. Her immediate fear of tempting them to commit some violation—as the one-time entry permit they held was issued specifically for a medical consultation at the Rabin Medical Center, which is not situated at the Tel Aviv beach—she kept to herself. For the mother and father and sister and brother urgently needed some solace, and after all one could say that too was a health issue under the circumstances. Relaxing on the shore of the blue sea, she thought, is just what they needed—and she did too, as a matter of fact. And Tel Aviv has many such beaches, with rather clean sand and pleasant promenades and cafés . . .

Oh, what a lovely day
Let's open our eyes
To the sun shining above

And the maddeningly blue sea . . .
And I'm just so, so, so happy (popular song)

And they rode her red Ford Fiesta to the shore of the blue sea.
The photograph shows Jamil and his sister standing at the
Tel Aviv beach: two handsome youngsters, slim, both in jeans,
his black, hers blue, he in a black hooded shirt with the image
of a bird spreading its wings over the word REBOX, with his
head uncovered, his curly hair cropped short, and she with
the traditional kerchief hiding her long hair, which otherwise
would flow down her back, soft and fragrant and pleasant to
the touch—the woman knew, for she had stroked that hair.
The two of them smile gently, but her eyes are sad, while he—
who was seeing the sea for the first time in his life—his eyes are
smiling too. Behind them is the expanse of the sea, rolling its
small waves after decorating them with a silver-foamy crown,
foam upon the water.
    That is the end of the story of Jamil's first encounter with the
sea. A second encounter was not expected soon, even though at
that time they did not imagine the walls that would soon close
him in and for many days expel even the dream of a second
encounter.

### Until the End of Proceedings: Jamil's Case

"In this case a ruling is issued of detention until the end of
proceedings," one of the military court records stipulated, the
court called Judea Court, situated at Ofer military base. The
case referred to is Jamil's, and unfortunately there was no way
of knowing when the proceedings in this case would end.
    Therefore Jamil's attorney appealed to revoke the ruling to

hold his client in custody until the end of proceedings and asked for him to be released on bail. About one month after Jamil's arrest, on March 19, the officer who acted as judge in this court, Captain Lior Kahana, ruled that his detention until the end of proceedings was unjustified. The reason was that the testimony of the key witness who incriminated him did not identify "any concrete facts relating to time or place implicating the accused person [namely Jamil] as belonging to the Popular Front for the Liberation of Palestine, and in fact he finds himself in a situation where he 'must prove he has no sister . . .'" The witness does not link the accused to any specific action, "does not specify when or how he joined the Front, in which parades he participated," nor do the two other witnesses for the prosecution "mention the accused as the person described in the action in which they partook."

Therefore Captain Lior Kahana ruled as follows:

> In view of the principles of Israeli law such incrimination cannot hold alongside principles of the presumption of innocence, a person's right to know the grounds on which he is charged, and the duty of the interrogating authorities to do everything within their power to get to the truth. Under the circumstances of the present interrogation, the accused did everything within his power namely to "deny that he has a sister" and to state that the incriminating witness is a bastard. . . . Added to the above statement there is a humanitarian circumstance regarding the severe medical condition of a close family member requiring the accused's presence at the Rabin Medical Center for a life-saving procedure for his sister. . . . I therefore rule hereby that the respondent will be detained but allowed to be released pending the following

conditions . . . The cash deposit of 10,000 shekels . . . the signature of two third-party guarantors for the sum of 10,000 shekels, one his father's . . . and the other, that of a friend of the family, Dr. Ilana Hammerman . . . The respondent is forbidden to leave his village.

When Jamil's father and the friend of the family who is presently writing the story exited the courtroom, holding a payment form and the bail deposit, the father was not sure he quite understood whether the news was good or bad:

"Is Jamil required to prove he has no sister?" he asked her.

"No," she answered, "it's a joke—for some reason that judge was kidding—and the news is excellent: Jamil will be freed on bail, perhaps even today, and will await trial at home. We'll deposit the money and that's that. Here's the form: 'The sum in words: ten thousand shekels only' is what it says, and I have ten thousand in my bank account. I'll go and deposit them and get the form stamped."

But she didn't go. For on that very day the military prosecution announced it was appealing against the ruling of release on bail. The form and its attached and unstamped stub remained in her hand, and Jamil remained in prison at Ofer.

After a while the prosecution's appeal was heard at a higher echelon, namely the "Military Court of Appeals." The officer acting as judge there held a higher rank too: lieutenant-colonel. It was Lieutenant Colonel Nathaniel Benichou, and he even bore the title Deputy Chief Justice.

The prosecution was represented by a young female officer named Jenia Wolinsky.

And thus spake Captain Wolinsky: "Even if other people do not name the respondent, they do not mention that he was *not* a member of the cell. Witness no. 2 for the prosecution mentions that the cell was writing slogans and participating in parades. Even if *no* activity was specified in that witness's testimony, there is extensive ruling on *insubstantial membership* that justifies detention until the end of proceedings. . . . I therefore request to reverse the previous court ruling."

Lieutenant Colonel Nathaniel Benichou accepted her request and reversed the ruling. He argued that the compatibility test for organ transplant for the ill sister could be held in detention as well. "Therefore," he concluded, "at this point I believe that public interest to prevent the risk that might result from releasing the appealer is greater than the harm that his detention might cause him and those close to him. These circumstances considered, I grant the prosecution's appeal and rule to keep him in detention until the end of proceedings."

And it was still impossible to tell when those proceedings would come to an end.

## Until the End of Proceedings: The Case of Yanai Lazla

Inspired by the legal term "until the end of proceedings," the friend of the family who is writing the story of Jamil wishes to deviate again from the main plot and recount part of another man's story. She does not know him in person but has no doubt that he deserves to be not merely another literary figure but the main protagonist of an entire life story, while at this stage Jamil was due only a short piece of writing about an episode in his life, one that also became a part of hers. A small part of Yanai Lazla's story is linked with Jamil's because his case was reviewed by the Israel Supreme Court in Jerusalem a few days after Jamil was sentenced to remain in prison, and therefore the friend of the family—who at the time was interested in the term "detention until the end of proceedings"—could learn from reading the press and later records of the trial that although that other man had committed very serious crimes, and was indeed convicted for them, *he* did not remain in custody until the end of the proceedings. The proceedings took a very long time in his case as well, much longer than in Jamil's, but even after his conviction he was allowed to return home, under house arrest.

Yanai Lazla was convicted for violations—crimes, to be more precise—that he committed in late 2002 while serving as a soldier in the Israeli Border Police at Hebron. His crimes were committed, as stated in his verdict, during "a premeditated spree of abuse and harassment of the [Palestinian] inhabitants in Hebron."

And here is the story of that premeditated spree, according to its exact description in one of the court protocols: Yanai Lazla and three of his fellow soldiers rode a military jeep through the streets of Hebron, grabbed two passersby and forced them into their jeep, took them to an isolated spot, and kicked and beat them there with a truncheon and rifle butts, seriously wounding and also robbing them. They then took another man into the jeep and threw him out as it sped on. This man was injured by his fall and limped away. Finally the four soldiers abducted a seventeen-year-old boy, 'Amran Abu Hamadiya. He was beaten up inside the jeep and then ordered to stand up and jump out. He stood in the rear of the jeep but refused to jump and held on to its top straps. His abductors forced his hands open, and he fell from the jeep moving at the speed of 80 km per hour— and was killed.

Or in the words of the Jerusalem District Court: "Unfortunately for the deceased, he ran into the defendant and his friends as they were on their killing rampage on December 30, 2002, and thus found his death."

Over five years later, in April 2008, the Jerusalem District Court sentenced Yanai Lazla to six and a half years in prison. Among his extenuating circumstances, the document refers to his mental instability and difficult family situation, including the condition of his sister who had been injured in a traffic accident and needed prolonged rehabilitation. Lazla, not arrested even after his conviction, did not report to serve his sentence and was regarded a "fugitive from detention."

Be that as it may, the State objected to the leniency of his sentence, and the Supreme Court, in its capacity as Criminal Court of Appeals, accepted the appeal. A high-flown and emotional ruling given on March 31, 2009—twelve days after the ruling to keep Jamil in prison—stated among other things that the "failure" of Lazla and his mates

> reflects in a nutshell the essential antithesis to the values of enlightened human society and to the values of generations of the Jewish People. . . . Such phenomena require an iron hand when punishing as soon as they occur in order to extricate them from our midst, so no trace of them is left. There is no mercy for a person who abuses his power and his weapon as an IDF soldier against an innocent helpless civilian because of the latter's ethnic origin, to the extent of taking his life. Extenuating circumstances should be considered on principle, but their relative weight diminishes as the horror of the committed act mounts. And in this case the horror and bestiality of the deeds are overriding.

The iron hand added two years to the prison sentence, resetting the sentence of the perpetrator of murder and harassment to eight and a half years of incarceration, and stipulated that this sentence was meant to reflect "the utter uniqueness of the crimes we have reviewed here . . . and relay a clear message of condemnation of such harassment that must never again be seen or heard in our midst."

The friend of the family who writes the story of Jamil read these documents shortly after Jamil was remanded until the end of proceedings, and her eyes captured the defense's demand in Yanai Lazla's trial to consider grounds for leniency in his sentence "and the lengthy house arrest under which he was placed during those proceedings." She thought about Jamil, who was not accused of any violence, and was not yet convicted for any violation whatsoever, and yet was not permitted house arrest but was rather consigned to prison until the end of proceedings.

## *(Ten) Years of Incarceration*

As anyone who is interested knows, one of the reasons for not keeping a detainee in custody until the end of legal proceedings is that the proceedings might last longer than his prison sentence in case of conviction. In Jamil's case, Captain Wolinsky—who, as noted, appealed against the ruling of the lower authorities to free him on bail, and opined that even "insubstantial membership" justifies detention until the end of proceedings—argued that the violations ascribed to Jamil were severe enough to merit a sentence of "ten years in prison."

"Ten years?" the lieutenant colonel asked the captain. Even he was somewhat taken aback. He must have whispered something to the court recorder, because the word "ten"—which the friend of the family heard with her own ears, and out of sheer amazement let out an embarrassing shout in the courtroom, which was empty of any other spectators except for Jamil's parents—was deleted from the protocol and the sentence remained cropped: "He will be sentenced to years in prison." Again the friend of the family thought of a comparison: (ten) years in prison for an insubstantial membership and attending an insubstantial meeting and writing insubstantial slogans, none of which could be proved—versus the eight-and-a-half-years prison sentence of a murderer and abuser whose acts were dated and documented by video camera.

Well, at that point Jamil could expect to be imprisoned for years. Jamil who had never shown any interest in political struggles and was entirely given to his private life, the focus of which at that time was his fervent love for a beautiful young woman who reciprocated—the two lovers had but one struggle in their lives: to obtain her reluctant parents' assent to their marriage; Jamil, who as a member of a conservative religious Muslim family could not imagine having any kind of ties with a secular leftist organization such as the Popular Front; Jamil, about whom during one of the numerous proceedings in his case the witness for the prosecution said he did not know him at all, and his name, known to the witness by rumor only, had been mentioned under the duress of interrogation and in the hope that the witness would be rewarded and freed to go home; Jamil, who since the very first court sessions had made clear he was the victim of a vague denunciation by other youngsters, the kind of false denunciation that occurs dozens of times every day under military rule.

Jamil then found himself in dire straits, for not only was he kept in custody until the end of proceedings but, far worse, innumerable cases like his raised the fear that neither the weak evidence against him nor the state of his sister's health would help, and the military court would rule that he too required an iron hand in punishment. That is, he really would be sentenced to "years in prison" so that no illegal parades or slogans would be seen or heard in our midst, neither concrete nor insubstantial.

## *In the Yard*

In the meantime proceedings dragged on, a month and another and yet another, and so the friend of the family who attended the proceedings became somewhat familiar with the yards at the Ofer military court, then eventually knew them inside out and even managed to bring about a modest change in one of them—very modest, tiny, minuscule.

This is how it went.

In this compound, consisting of a large prison pen enclosed by concentric fences and walls with entry from the outer fence only through electrical turnstiles, one after the other, that receive only authorized, checked, and approved persons between their iron bars after each has left behind all personal effects and deposited his or her ID with the guards. One is allowed into the next area beyond the turnstiles only after a body search inside a small cubicle. Here any woman wearing a hijab is required to remove all the decorative pins that attach the various folds of that head garment to each other with beautiful precision, and throw them into the waste bin, so there is no chance that she can commit a terrorist stabbing. So women come out of that compartment somewhat disheveled, sometimes even with a rebellious strand of hair showing on their perspiring woman foreheads.

In this compound, then, the large prison pen contained a smaller fenced-in one, and in the latter were a waiting room and another yard. The friend of the family noticed that passing through the smaller pen's barbed-wire fence, right after exiting the body-search cubicles, were all the Palestinians who were allowed to come here—namely two family members of each detainee whose case was to be reviewed that day by one of the military court's echelons. At first she thought they entered the place of their own free will, for she saw no sign or written order for them to do so, but she later found out that their will is not a deciding factor here, for whenever any of them exited without an attorney gesturing or calling out their names to come into the review of his or her family member's case, the guards ordered them back inside. Only detainees' family members entered— all Palestinians—and not the Israeli women and men and the few international women and men who regularly attended the place on behalf of human rights organizations, and not even the attorneys in their white shirts and black trousers and their large briefcases, who spoke to their detained clients' relatives by approaching the fence of the smaller pen and speaking through it. Because of this, she thought it was not merely the duty of Palestinians to remain there but it was also their right, their exclusive right, and all the rest were denied it. Whether duty or right, however, she found this separation strange, though she was used to the separation normally made in her country between Palestinians and non-Palestinians, and especially between them and Jews; but the gate of this particular separation barrier was not locked. Most of the time it stood wide open, and still everyone respected it, and those who were separated did not intermingle.

For a long while she too respected it and stood, like the attorneys, outside the fence and spoke through it with those on its other side, with Jamil's family members and sometimes with others. They had many hours to spend talking like this. These were not vacation days, but she and the family members had never had so much time on their hands, since one could never tell exactly when the court session would take place, whether at 9:00 a.m. or at 4:00 p.m. or any time in between. They often waited almost all of those seven hours.

One day, as the hours dragged on, the friend of the family got tired of standing by the fence and resolved to enter the unlocked gate and continue the conversation in the waiting room, where many chairs were visible through the open door. And she entered and saw that it was good—no one ordered her out, and there was even a kiosk counter for buying sweets and black coffee in paper cups. Thus from then on the conversations took place under a roof where the conversation partners could sit, munch wafers, and sip coffee.

But the waiting room was faded and dreary, and therefore those who were waiting sometimes felt like breathing some fresh air under the blue sky as they quietly and calmly drank their coffee, and so from time to time they would go out to the yard. However, the yard had no benches, forcing them to stand—that is to say, most of them stood, but several elderly men and women got tired of standing and sat down on the ground, although this was somewhat undignified for elderly people. The friend of the family—who sometimes got tired and sat down with them—thought they deserved to have at least mats to sit on, or rather mats strewn with cushions to lean on.

Gradually the family friend also noticed that on the other side of the fence, in the part of the compound that was nearly empty, holding only attorneys, and guards pacing up and down, while the human rights activists stationed themselves in the courtrooms to listen to the hearings, there was normal seating. These seats were connected in twos and threes and were always vacant. So she suggested to the people standing with her that they pass through the open gate in the fence and bring those seats back with them to their own area, which she also had come to consider her own, although they made up an absolute national majority and she a minority of one.

Minority? She was one single Jew among Arabs. Here, by the way, is the place to mention that to this day she can't understand why for all those months the human rights advocates did not come in to speak with family members of the Palestinian detainees. For she found many interlocutors among them—after all, everyone there was bored to death—and greatly expanded her geographic and human acquaintance with the West Bank, from Nablus in the north to Yatta in the south.

But the tale she wishes to tell here is of the tiny change she made. Since her suggestion to go out and bring in the seats to their area was not immediately accepted—people were obviously apprehensive about it—she got up to try it on her own. And since she did not have the strength required to drag them more than a few paces, some of the men present got up and gave her a hand, or to be more exact she let go and they dragged. Within a few moments, several of the attached seats were standing in the small inner yard, and some of those sitting on the ground got up and sat down on them.

The guards looked on and smiled. One of them did ask her who gave her permission to initiate the moving around of military equipment, and demanded that she go to the commander to seek permission. She answered that nothing made better sense than moving seats from a place where there was no demand for them to a place where there was, and therefore permission could be taken for granted. The guard did not persist, and his smile grew broad. And then for a while amused and smiling faces were seen on both sides of the fence, as though everyone was of one company, a group of innocents enclosed by fences.

The seats remained in place for months, and more seats were added. For a while the friend of the family got some satisfaction out of this, but just as earlier she had grown tired of standing, she eventually grew tired of the endless sitting around, and since unlike the Palestinians enclosed in the inner pen within the larger pen she was allowed to come and go at will among the various pens and enter the courtrooms, she began to join the human rights advocates to spend some of her hours at Ofer listening to reviews of other defendants' cases.

## *In the Courtroom*

Ofer military court consists of several pavilions, all of which look alike, all of them rectangular, all of them whitewashed, all of them a little above ground level, and each of them has a front door with a small metal staircase leading up to it, and left of this staircase is a partition behind which the defendants are brought in, invisibly, through the rear door.

Every pavilion contains a courtroom. It is modestly designed but clean and efficient. A wooden partition divides it in two. In its front part the court session is conducted with a podium for the judge, tables for the prosecution, the defense, and the witnesses, a table for the interpreter, a stand for whoever is speaking in turn—and a defendant's dock. Usually several defendants sit there, in order not to delay the next hearing—a bit like waiting for the doctor at certain very organized clinics, where the person who is next is summoned to enter an inner waiting room like a baseball player on deck. In the back part of the courtroom are several wooden benches for the public.

And that is the issue here concerning the public: although the court is a military one, its courtrooms do contain an audience, attesting to the fact that even here justice is not only done but also witnessed. This is also evident in the clause "Publicity in judicial proceedings," amendments 8, 10, and 32 of the "Order on Security Regulations no. 378," clause 11(a), of which the following clarifications are iterated regarding any issue, from security to morality and the welfare of children and witnesses:

> A military court will hold its sessions open to the public; however, a military court may order its session to be conducted entirely or partially behind closed doors if it deems it necessary on grounds of ensuring the security of IDF troops, public security, protection of morality or the welfare of a minor, or if it finds that a session open to the public might deter a witness from testifying freely or at all.

Court hearings, then, are open to the public by official order, and indeed only rarely was the friend of Jamil's family aware of a decision to hold any session behind closed doors—the sessions were public even when the defendants were minors or when witnesses were obviously afraid to testify. However, whether because Ofer is distant from any community and because of its walls and fences and the meticulous inspectors at its gates who enable only family members to attend—as written above, two for each defendant—and for some unknown reason prevent Israeli citizens from entering, or because public interest in the court hearings there is negligible at best, no members of the public attend the military court at Ofer.

So the front benches meant for the public are always almost vacant, while the family members, for whom this is a rare opportunity to see the defendant, always sit on the back bench, as far as possible from their loved one, who sits with chained feet in the dock in the front part of the courtroom. This detail greatly surprised the friend of the family, until she noticed that if family members did move up to one of the front benches during the hearing, they were ordered back to the rear, and from there they sometimes tried to exchange signs and gestures with the defendant, or even a few words. She on the other hand was allowed to sit wherever she pleased, and might even move from one place to another in order to see better.

In this way she managed to exchange a few words with Jamil, for during his court hearing she sat not far from him and at times even approached and stood beside him until one of the guards—who first stared at her curiously—ordered her away.

That was how she heard from Jamil about the containers. He told her that when a court session was scheduled, he was brought from prison early in the morning, and during the long hours that she and his relatives spent waiting outside for his session, he and other detainees—so he complained—waited inside a closed container, a suffocating space, and received neither food nor drink there.

She later went to look for these containers and found them behind a barbed-wire fence beyond the last pavilion. They had been actually visible the whole time, but until some face emerged behind their closely barred small windows, one couldn't have imagined that they were used for storing not equipment but people. When their turn comes, these people are taken out and marched into one of the pavilions and into the courtroom where their case is reviewed.

When the friend of the family entered the courtroom where the case of one of these people was to be reviewed, she discovered that the prosecutor was the very same Jenia Wolinsky who had demanded that Jamil remain in custody until the end of proceedings. The family friend sat down to listen alertly to that court session and felt some satisfaction upon seeing that Captain Wolinsky was not so lucky here, as the two witnesses for the prosecution claimed they didn't remember what exactly happened that long-gone day when, according to the bill of indictment, the defendant was one of two persons firing guns during a demonstration.

The first witness, a young man who had been tried and convicted for arms trading, and whom the prosecution summoned from prison to testify that he had given a weapon to the defendant, said he had never had any contact with the defendant and knew him superficially simply because both were residents of the same refugee camp. The prosecutor attempted in vain to coax him to admit that he had given the defendant a weapon, as he had said in a previous interrogation. Finally she turned to Major Menachen Lieberman, who sat in judgment at this session, and asked to declare him a "hostile witness." Major Menachem Lieberman agreed, which meant there was still a chance for her to gain something from that earlier incriminating testimony.

The second witness's testimony went even worse for her. He too was a convicted prisoner and party to the shooting discussed in the hearing. And although no one was injured by the gunfire in that demonstration, he had been sentenced to a lengthy prison term, eight years, nearly as many as Yanai

Lazla. This prisoner, unfortunately for the present defendant, had named him at the time as the second gunman. However, he now retracted and claimed adamantly that he did not remember who the second gunman was and that he had named the present defendant just in order to name someone, anyone, because he was desperate to bring an end to his lengthy interrogation. Captain Wolinsky appealed to declare him a "hostile witness" as well so that his original accusation would still have some weight.

As the session wore on, Major Menachem Lieberman had refined his rocking motions on the large black seat, occasionally embellishing them with a stretching of arms and huge yawns. This time he denied the prosecution's request. The friend of the family noticed that between yawns he generally played his role well in this show: the role of an objective judge, aloof and superior and above political considerations, who truly wished, with great patience, although rather indifferent and mocking and not particularly attentive, to help all those involved to arrive at the truth of an alleged terrorist shooting that had taken place five or six years earlier during one of the numerous demonstrations held almost daily at the outskirts of Qalandiya refugee camp.

At one point, perhaps because the event was given the charged name "terrorist shooting," Major Menachem Lieberman, who a moment earlier had concentrated on picking a hair from his jacket and carefully examining it, shook himself into full engagement. Using a series of details and gestures he explained to the young female officer, apparently utterly ignorant in matters of weapons and gunfire, various techniques of firing in the air and not in the air, at a distant checkpoint or at persons nearby. Then when the witness called what went on at the demonstration "a child's game," the major became a bit annoyed, which was unlike him, and dismissed the witness's words with the wave of a hand, almost with revulsion, although the witness had been declared "not hostile."

"We were children at the time, crazy," said the young man in answer to the defense attorney's question.

"Was the basic purpose of this shooting to kill Jewish people?" asked the defense attorney.

"No," the witness answered.

"The purpose was to play games?" the defense attorney asked.

"Yes, we were simply excited to be shooting," the witness answered.

And that was how the questioning ended. The defense attorney had no further questions. The prosecutor did have some questions about that shooting—"terrorist shooting" was what she called it now that it had become very clear what kind of people this court was dealing with. Did they cherish the illusion that the court would accept the argument that shooting is a children's game intended only to fire in the air and not injure Jewish people? But Captain Wolinsky did not prolong her arguments either, for the time was nearly noon—that is, lunchtime. The session had yielded only meager results. The judge announced when the next session would take place, in two or three weeks' time, or a month (the friend of the family no longer recalls), and got up and left. The defendant's family members tried to approach him on their way out, his mother even reached out her hand to touch him, but a guard was in the way. The young man was handcuffed and rapidly removed through the back door and returned to his detention until the end of proceedings.

## *The Story of Jamil: Ending*

In the meantime proceedings in Jamil's case also continued at the pace of two or three weeks or a month apart. Finally, however, a dramatic development took place, or rather several dramatic developments.

On November 5, 2009—Jamil had already spent almost nine months in prison by then—Major Hilit Bar-On-Bieber, now sitting in judgment on his case, gave her verdict and ruled that "the defendant is to be acquitted on grounds of doubt about the three violations ascribed to him in the bill of indictment."

Jamil was to be freed that very day.

However, that day the military prosecution requested that his release be postponed so that prosecution could consider an appeal. The judge agreed to this request and delayed his release by seventy-two hours.

During those three days the prosecution deliberated and resolved to lodge an appeal and indeed did so, not only an appeal but also a request to extend detention until a verdict be delivered by the appeals court.

Two more days passed, and on November 10, 2009, Lieutenant Colonel Aharon Mishnayot, who acted as judge in the Military Court of Appeals at Ofer, rejected the request to extend detention, among other reasons because he doubted the appeal's chances of success. He instructed that Jamil be released pending the conditions set by the court as early as March of that year: a cash deposit of 10,000 shekels, the signature of two third-party guarantors for 10,000 shekels each, confinement to his village, etc. This time bail was posted that very day, the stub was stamped and handed over at some counter, and Jamil was free to go home.

After a while came the appeal hearing. Suddenly for some

reason its chances for success increased: on that day, after long hours during which the friend of the family waited with Jamil and his father in that smaller courtyard next to the waiting room inside the larger fenced-in yard, the smaller yard that still had benches, the defense attorney came out and told them that unfortunately the officer now sitting in judgment was Lieutenant Colonel Nathaniel Benichou, who as we know had earlier agreed to the prosecution's request and extended Jamil's detention. This time too he was favorably inclined toward the prosecution, and therefore Jamil might have to return to prison for a lengthy term.

Hearing this, the friend of the family recalled those "(ten) years in prison." And perhaps Jamil too remembered them, for after adamantly refusing for so long to admit to any guilt, he became very dispirited—his young face went ashen—and he gave in and assented to the proposal which Benichou made, that he sign a plea bargain and avoid another session.

And these were the details of the plea bargain proposed by Benichou: Jamil was to plead guilty as charged on all counts and would be convicted of membership in an illegal organization, presence at a certain assembly, participation in parades celebrating the founding of that organization, writing slogans of that organization, etc. All of this had supposedly occurred since 2006 or thereabouts until the time of his arrest. His guilty plea would incur the following penalties: effective imprisonment of eight months and twenty-two days, or precisely the duration of his detention, and another prison sentence of two years and a half suspended for two years, as well as a fine of 5,000 shekels to be deducted from his deposit.

Jamil signed, having pleaded guilty as charged, was convicted—and went home.

## *Epilogue*

Finally the love of Jamil and the beautiful young woman with whom he was enamored and who reciprocated overcame all the obstacles that circumstances placed before them for another five years, and they got married. Their first son, born prematurely, grew into a healthy baby and now toddles around, soon to be celebrating his second birthday.

Jamil's sister underwent successful transplant surgery with her father's liver lobe and kidney, and is presently studying English at the university. But that's another story, with a happy ending, for the time being.

# The Story of the Invisible Ones

## *People*

It was late morning. At one end of the long corridor, its walls clad handsomely with rough bright Jerusalem stone, the back of a thin figure was seen for a while, in a brown shirt and trousers, both quite baggy. This person stood facing the wall, ankles chained to one another. A large man in a dark gray uniform, with shiny metal shackles, a bunch of keys, and a walkie-talkie all attached to his belt, approached the figure and silently turned it a little. Now one could see the handcuffs on the thin wrists, the same kind of shackles the large man carried on his belt, and the face half-hidden behind huge black eyeglasses, opaque, blank.

It was the face of a boy, judging by his smooth cheeks. His lips were pursed tight as the hands holding him turned him around some more and gently pushed him back, into a niche in the narrow wall at the end of the corridor with a step below. His feet bumped into the step and his lips opened, his face tilted up a bit, frozen in blind surprise. The silent man in the gray

uniform pressed down on his shoulders, squeezing his body
not roughly but firmly, to make him sit on the step. The boy's
body resisted at first, stiffened, then let go, bent slowly, leaning
slightly backwards, resisted again, and tried to find some balance, compensating for the backward tilt by leaning forward
against the hands pressing down on his shoulders, and finally
surrendering and letting his behind drop to the step, landing
with a slight thump. Now the pusher's equilibrium was lost
for a moment as the thin body dropped out of his grip, but
he straightened up and looked with satisfaction at the seated
boy, whose fingers began fumbling with the fabric of his brown
trousers. The boy might have calmed down from the moves
forced on him by the man—made invisible to him by the black
eyeglasses—and he might even have found a comfortable position but for a brown security door in the white corridor with
a modest plaque saying "Briefing Room." Just then this door
opened, and a man wearing a large blue skullcap appeared in
the doorway, his face unshaven and his jeans and a sweater
faded and a bit shabby. He gestured to the gray-uniformed man
to bring in his ward. The large hands that had pressed down
were now thrust in the sitter's armpits to pull him up and then
directed the boy, who had gotten up faster than he had sat
down, toward the open door, pushing him lightly, still in total
silence, until he stood in the doorway. There a different pair of
hands, gentler this time, reached toward his face and removed
the large black eyeglasses, but before the boy's face was fully visible the door closed and the brown-clad boy vanished behind it.

   Opposite the closed door another security door now opened,
and behind it yet another, of cream-colored metal with a small
barred window, and from that door another figure was pushed
into the corridor with its ankles chained together and hand-

cuffed and the top half of its face hidden behind large opaque eyeglasses, and it too stood for a moment facing the wall, its back to the corridor.

To judge by the span of his shoulders, this was the back of a sturdy, full-grown young man. He was not wearing brown prisoner garb but was dressed instead with domestic casualness in a wide yellowish knit top of unclear cut and mouse-colored sweatpants, and had his hands been free he would certainly have pulled up the pants and tried to tuck their elastic belt under the knit top as the belt was worn down in some places where the stitches had come apart. And perhaps he would have laced up his blue sneakers, which were quite loose with their tongues hanging down to the sides, their bright orange belly exposed. But no, even with free hands he could not have laced them, for the holes were devoid of any laces, and perhaps he didn't even care about his open and exposed shoes and the pants that were practically slipping off his hips and exposing a strip of green briefs, just as the fat man with the blue skullcap apparently didn't care about not shaving that morning or about the unbecoming and unmatched clothes he wore or indeed about his whole crumpled and wan person.

Nor did the army officer care, sitting in the room behind the door into which the boy was led and after a short while taken back out of it with his eyes and almost his entire nose covered by the opaque glasses again. Then she, the woman standing in the corridor and observing all of this, was allowed to enter and view the short legal proceedings that took place in that room publicly and in the presence of all parties, according to the protocols printed at the end of every hearing. The army officer sat clean-shaven and relaxed at a table, and his graying hair made him seem trustworthy, very civilian like in spite of his senior rank: lieutenant colonel. Neither did he seem to mind biting the nails of two of his fingers in public and in full view of the parties and the few others present; he was perfectly content to bite them at his leisure, not a sign of nerves. But none of this seemed important to the parties, although one of them, the defense attorney, was surprisingly clean-shaven—like the officer who acted as judge in this court—and almost elegant in his dark blue suit over a starched and ironed blue shirt and matching necktie, and one could imagine he gave off the fragrance of a men's luxury perfume which perhaps one might have discerned had the room not been filled with a noticeable smell, probably coming from the corridor leading to the other corridor clad with handsome stone or perhaps from the detainee cells lining it, where many fingers were clutching the iron bars of their doors when the woman who came to see all these things made her way past them to this room marked Briefing Room. This term did not suggest that it served as a modest venue for a military court, one of the military courts of the Judea and Samaria District, as announced by a sign in both Hebrew and Arabic fixed on one of the walls inside, which was also decorated by two Israeli flags and a copper plaque with the relief of olive branches on both sides of a menorah (seven-branched candelabra), Israel's official emblem.

In this room that day the army officer who acted as judge in this court, just like other senior officers like him on other days there, was required to extend the detention of those who had stood blindfolded and shackled facing the wall of the handsomely tiled corridor. They were delivered here one after another, and their opaque eyeglasses were removed upon entry and the shackles on their wrists unlocked, each shackle separately, and the detainees—most of them very young, some looking like children—froze for a moment, their arms dangling down, gazed, blinking, straight ahead or sideways, and then shook their feet a bit along with the six-link chain that connected them at the ankles. One might have expected them to immediately smooth out their clothes, but none of them did, perhaps because they were very soon required to sit on a pale wooden bench and then immediately ordered to rise again—sometimes at the order "All rise!" and sometimes just with a slight hand gesture of the man who had brought them into the room—in honor of the judge.

The officer who acted as judge in this court that day turned a friendly face to the detainees brought in before him one by one, perhaps ten of them, or maybe eleven or twelve: he looked directly at each of them and bade him good morning in Arabic. Then he read his name from the white folder placed open in front of him and asked him in Hebrew to confirm that he was indeed the person named. Everyone did, except for one, detainee number 6, who shook his head and murmured a different name and was immediately taken out and exchanged for another. The officer smiled at all the rest and signaled graciously to them to sit down again, and then, in every single proceeding, a mild exchange took place for some minutes between the necktied defense attorney standing at one side of the table and the man in jeans and sweater and large blue skullcap at the other side, whom the records named "investigator," who acted as prosecutor in this court.

This exchange, judging by the growing indifference and fatigue of the parties as well as of the officer-judge and court recorder at his side, hidden behind an outdated computer screen, unfolded in a manner exceedingly familiar to all of them. Often both questions and answers were worded exactly alike, with only the first question answered differently each time: when was my client arrested, the defense attorney would begin, and the investigator-prosecutor would give the date. Hearing the date the first few times, the watching woman tried to calculate how long the youngster seated on the bench at that moment—between the soldier or policeman or prison guard holding the shiny shackles and those strange black eyeglasses and the interpreter, an adolescent who at times murmured the questions and answers in his ear, in Arabic—how long has the detainee been kept in detention: days? weeks? months? Eventually she learned that even this variable was not necessarily personal nor of any relevance to the legal proceeding, for the protocol she read of a proceeding she had witnessed on February 11, 2008, said that the detainee was arrested on February 14, 2008—three days past that day.

In fact, very few other matters were cleared up by the questions and answers that followed. The defense attorney wished to know who interrogated his client: police? Shabak (security services)? perhaps both? He usually received a clear answer: sometimes the one, sometimes the other, and on occasion both. But as the parties proceeded to the subsequent script for their roles, nothing else that was concrete could be learned: one asked what the interrogators had gleaned from their interrogations, and his colleague (between hearings the woman who came to see and hear all these things realized the Palestinian defense attorney and the Israeli investigator-prosecutor did treat each other as colleagues, these two, tapping each other on the back and joking in fluent Arabic and in Hebrew) would answer him in the very same manner or with slight changes: *I am prevented from specifying*, he would say over and over, and in his third or fourth or fifth repetition he might switch to *I cannot answer*, or *I am prevented from answering*. At times he would declare more exactly, *I cannot go into the details of the interrogation*, and look at the judge and say: *The confidential report contains the details, your honor may read the report,* and look back at the defense attorney and say to him, *Confidential material with details of the interrogation has been provided,* but skip the "your honor may," etc. And again to the judge: *I direct your attention to the confidential report.* And his voice did not inflect either up nor down, it neither hesitated nor broke but was mechanically ready for questions presented by the other party, also monotonous, flat, perhaps still inflecting upward toward the end to suggest the interrogative mode, but often not even that, until at times one could not tell with any certainty whether the defense attorney was asking or stating:

My client is suspected of being a member of an organization
Yes.
What did he divulge
I am prohibited from specifying this.
He confessed
Partly, other counts he denies.
The investigation is getting somewhere
We are certainly not where we started.
Is it a matter of arms trade?
There's suspicion of that as well.
But you haven't really got anything of the kind, right.
We haven't.
What are you interrogating the suspect for then?
To get to the truth.
Is the suspect cooperating with his interrogators?
I cannot answer in detail. It might impact the investigation
    at this point.

And so on and so forth, for a moment or two or three, until suddenly, who knows why now, the defense attorney announces:

*I have no further questions!* and the dialogue is thus concluded
to the satisfaction of all those present. The silence following his
announcement shakes everyone into a semblance of life and
motion—the detainee raises his head a little; the interpreter
moves away from him, stretches his limbs, and makes himself
comfortable on the bench; the guard handles the shackles and
black eyeglasses which will soon be returned to their places on
wrists and face; and after another moment the keyboard again
clicks under the fingertips of the court recorder, and the judge's
voice rings out: *Ruling!*

The interpreter squares his shoulders and tells the detainee,
*Qarar!* The judge announces his ruling as follows:

> After hearing both parties and reading the confidential re-
> port and the investigation presented to me, it is my opinion
> that there is good reason to believe the suspect may have
> committed the acts which are the subject of this investi-
> gation and therefore it must be allowed to continue to its
> completion; still I rule hereby that the detainee be held in
> custody for only eleven more days.

This ruling too is announced and received in total indifference, for all those involved are familiar with its content from
the start. The ruler (the officer-judge) knows; the party requesting the ruling knows; the "investigating authorities" and their
representative, the investigator who acts as prosecutor in this
proceeding, knows; and the party opposing the request, the defense attorney, knows. Even the object of this ruling stipulating
where and how long he will be spending the coming days or
weeks—the detainee—knows.

This became obvious to the woman after she had carefully

followed three or four such proceedings. Unlike the rest of those present, she became especially alert every time the word "Ruling!" sounded and was even somewhat comforted by a certain tone of conciliation in the version that shortened the duration of detention: "Still . . . held in custody . . . for only . . ." But at the fourth or fifth proceeding she realized that here too a regular pattern was used: $Y-7 = X$.

In other words, if the anonymous investigating authorities requested thirty days, they would obtain an extension of only twenty-three. If they asked for another twenty-two days, they would get fifteen, and if they sought another eighteen days they would get eleven. And the phrase always began with "Still . . ." and ended with "for only . . . days."

That was how things unfolded that day and every other time the woman who came to see and hear in order to tell witnessed those proceedings. At the end of one particular hearing her ears pricked up when the major who was acting as judge surprised her. This time, after calling out "Ruling!" he began to review in detail the numerous days of detention that had been added in previous hearings.

"Proper practice," he said, "would be to aim for brief detention in order to enable proper supervision of the investigation," and he declared, "The court must in every way protect the right of the persons under investigation and especially when the detainee is denied meetings with an attorney." He went on: "As a rule, in such cases one must shorten the period of detention in order to enable tight supervision by the judiciary." There were more assertive and detailed statements in this vein, with reference to numerous legal precedents complete with names and numbers, sounding highly professional. He was evidently familiar with the art of rhetoric, for he injected his long monologue with pauses to ensure that the text on the computer screen was a faithful record of everything he had said and quietly instructing the court recorder to correct things here and there. At times his lips rubbed against each other and he looked at his small silent audience with the satisfaction of one who appreciates the power and attraction of narrative tension even in rather dry legal proceedings.

By now the woman, seated in that small silent audience, was convinced that this long monologue could not possibly end like all the other proceedings, and therefore when the familiar phrase "Still . . . held in custody for only eighteen more days" was pronounced at the end, she was taken aback. For a moment she could not help but be impressed with the major's literary sophistication—his speech had been a rather clever trick, she thought.

But she realized immediately that if there was any cleverness it had impressed no one but herself, for around her the audience faces were just as tired and bored as before. The pale, blank face of the detainee showed no signs of surprise or even disappointment as he got up and held out his hands to the shackles and his face to the black eyeglasses and let himself be dragged out of the room by his clothes as the black eyeglasses hid from him the next detainee. This next boy passed him with his eyes already uncovered and his hands held out to the prison guard to unlock the metal shackles, and was quickly seated on the bench, and rose and sat down again, and the defense attorney asked, *when was he arrested*, and the investigator-prosecutor replied, *on such and such a date*—and the defense attorney: *was he given the police version?*—and the investigator-prosecutor: *no, not yet*—and the defense attorney: *he has been held by the Shabak from his arrest until today, right?*—and the investigator-prosecutor:

*right*—and the defense attorney: *any convictions?*—and the investigator-prosecutor: *I am prevented from specifying at this point*—and so on and so forth until the ruling was spoken with the usual phrases: "Having heard . . . there is reason to believe that the suspect must be allowed . . . still . . . only . . . days."

## Doors

Once, however, a slight surprise of a different nature took place in that room: a moment before the detainee whose review had ended turned to hold out his hands to the shackles, the investigator-prosecutor leaped up and pointed down, calling loudly: *Look, a mouse! There's a mouse here! Look, it's running over there! Look, under the door!* And a real commotion broke out: all eyes turned to a closed metal door in the wall behind the investigator-prosecutor, and the defense attorney and the investigator-prosecutor exchanged some amused words about mice in general and the mice running around this room lately in particular, while the woman who had come to see and hear in order to tell and write fixed her eyes on the door under which the mouse apparently squeezed itself out and disappeared, a large door painted a creamy color, and realized to her amazement that until that moment she had not noticed this door at all, although she had gazed around that small room so often. Now her failure to notice a door annoyed her and led her to mentally count the many similar doors she remembered seeing every time she had walked the corridors of that building, doors that were mostly closed so there was no knowing where they led, so that finally her eye did not notice them at all, just as it had failed to register that door under which the mouse escaped that day.

"First door on the left," she had been told by one of the attorneys sitting in the handsomely tiled corridor, waiting for the detainee whom he represented to be led inside. He said this and turned toward the tiled wall behind him and knocked on it: "Right here behind us. The first door on the left, investigation wing." This was one of the short, fragmented answers he unwillingly gave when she tried to find out where they were brought from and where they were later taken, these people, two of whom were standing not far away, in a corner, pressed against the wall, shackled and unseeing. She pointed them out to the attorney and asked whether he knew why most of them looked so awful, pale and exhausted and blinking a lot, as she saw inside the "Briefing Room" turned courtroom. "Because they are held in solitary confinement with no window, no air, no sunlight, only a bad kind of neon light." And he too blinked but did not answer her when she asked whether that neon light was too strong or too weak.

She wouldn't let up: "How do you know?"

"Because I've been there," he answered.

"Can you visit your clients there?" she asked.

"No," he answered.

"So how come you were there?" she asked.

"Under investigation. I was interrogated. For twenty-one days. It was long ago. They let me go. Didn't find anything," he answered, and that was the longest sentence he said to her, and also the last.

First door on the left, she memorized, and when she exited the handsomely tiled corridor into the other corridor, its walls covered only with simple gray ceramic tiles, she passed several detention cells and noticed an iron door on the left. She approached it, and to her surprise the door stood open. Just a crack. She pushed it a little and took a cautious peep inside: another corridor, very short. Was this where the interrogation rooms were? More detention cells? Were the detainees brought out from there? She dared not enter to peep through the little window she noticed at the end of that short corridor, but drew back fearfully and without thinking returned the door to its previous position, open just a crack. The woman who comes from the outside to see and hear, and then tell others who do not come here, glanced sideways to see if anyone had noticed what she was doing against the rules of this place.

But no one noticed her at that moment, even though two men were right beside her. She had already seen one of them before, when she went out into the corridor, and she feared him: a man in uniform, perhaps a policeman, or a soldier or a privately employed security guard—an untrained eye could not distinguish between the different kinds of uniforms in this place (once she even saw a shackled detainee bundled up in a padded jacket belonging to an Israeli policeman). But this uniformed man did not scold her, probably because he was busy trying to push another man against the wall. This man, who had earlier hidden behind a partially opened door that was now closed, was a slight presence, bowed down, very close to the wall, arms hidden in front, black head of hair pressed by the back strap of the familiar opaque eyeglasses: a black stripe between two gray ones. Looking down, she saw the open laceless sneakers with tongues hanging out, before the door opened again and its iron wing closed upon the figure and made it vanish.

This was not the first time she had sighted this in the corridors she passed on her way to and from the "Briefing Room": a door standing wide open and then suddenly closed by someone on the other side, and a bit of corridor wall that is thus exposed and exposing the back of a person standing in the exposed corridor while the policeman in charge of that person immediately tried to minimize his presence. For an outsider it's a shocking, unpleasant, even outrageous sight, and this time she decided to speak to the guard.

"Why do you keep the detainees blindfolded as they wait for their court session?" she asked him. "After all, there's nothing to see here."

He shrugged. He was a tall fellow, his hair and complexion light and his facial features chiseled and handsome.

"Can't you speak?" She looked directly into his blue eyes.

"No," he answered and shrugged again. He added, "I have my instructions," leaning against the door that hid the detainee behind.

"But if their eyes are covered anyway, why do you make them all face the wall?" she asked.

"I can't answer you," he answered.

"Do you know why?" she asked.

"I do, but I am not allowed to answer you," he answered.


"Do you know why the detainees are kept that way before being brought into court—blindfolded, behind doors, pushed inside corners and facing walls?" she later asked the major who acted as judge that day in the room serving as a military courtroom, when the pause between two court sessions grew long.

"No," he answered, and was not at all cross with the question and even gave her a grounded answer, with that same goodwill that he exhibited, like many of his colleagues, when sitting in judgment: "I don't know because it is not within my jurisdiction. I am here inside this room the whole time. I am not supposed to look into what takes place behind this door. There is a division of responsibility here. I am judge, and not responsible for procedures at the detention facility. But the commander of this facility is a friend of mine, we served in the army together, and as soon as I'm done here I'll give him a call and ask him personally about the complaint we just heard from another detainee, about being beaten during his interrogation. Just so you don't think I don't care about what happens to these people."

And perhaps he really did care, that major, for not only did he bid every single detainee good morning but he also turned to others and asked them how they were. "I don't feel well," the interpreter translated the answer of one of those addressed. "I am cold in my cell. I am postsurgery. I need to see a doctor." The major gave him a kind look and explained that he was not responsible for the conditions at the detention facility. "I'm sorry," he said, turning the palms of his hands up, fingers splayed, signaling he was helpless. He really couldn't help in these matters, he could only make sure the complaints were recorded in the protocols, and he would also request that the detainee be referred to a doctor, and perhaps he could also request that his cell be heated, yes. Why not—let them heat the cell.

Another detainee who answered the major's question regarding his well-being said that he was very tired, that he was being interrogated all the time and not allowed to sleep. The major told this detainee too that he was sorry to hear that, but it was not within his jurisdiction, really not, he emphasized, pressing a hand to his heart, but he would record the complaint in protocol. And indeed this complaint was not only recorded but most likely looked into and denied, for the ruling the major read at the end of the session also said that "the suspect's claim of being deprived of sleep during interrogation is not

congruent with the times listed in the memoranda," and thus
the woman who had come to see and hear learned that every
single interrogation resulted in a memorandum, and the interrogators recorded the time the interrogation began and ended,
and thus the major—who took some time to leaf through the
confidential report in the complaining detainee's file—could
satisfy himself regarding the matter. Yet on that day another
detainee was looking so poorly and having such a hard time
standing steadily and answering the major who acted here as
judge and inquired after his well-being, that the major excused
him from standing and instructed protocol that this detainee
was to be referred to a doctor urgently.

In fact most of the youngsters the woman saw in corridors or on
the bench in the "Military Courtroom" at this detention facility
in the heart of Jerusalem, the place popularly named "Russian
Compound," didn't look too well. Generally they did not look
really ill, hungry, or beaten up, but they appeared faded and
wiped out. Yes, *faded* and *wiped out* are the words that best
describe these youngsters, as though someone had wiped their
faces clean of any color or expression, extinguished any spark
in their eyes, and drained their spines of their erect and supple
nature as they stood, walked, and sat.

## Solitary Confinement Cells and Interrogation Rooms

Wiped out, extinguished, drained. The detainees are held in
this detention facility in the heart of the city of Jerusalem for
two, three, four weeks and sometimes even longer, without a
moment of sunlight or a breath of fresh air, some or most of

the time alone inside a rectangular solitary confinement cell one meter by two, or a square cell two meters by two, containing a bed and two blankets, a small sink. and a hole in the floor to urinate and defecate in filth and stench. These cells are gray and have no windows, and they are equipped with an air-conditioning unit that blows chilly air into these small closed spaces, lit by feeble fluorescent light.

Yes, the light is too weak, not too strong. This detail, like the size of the cells and the air-conditioning issue and the filth and other details of prison cells from which and to which those shabby figures are taken after they are pushed blindfolded against walls and doors in corridors leading to the room serving as a military court—this is what the woman found out awhile later in Bethlehem, where she drove to meet two people who had been detained at the time in this detention facility. They described for her the interrogations and the interrogation rooms and the detention cells, and the physical and mental breakdown of those held there for long periods.


The interrogation rooms are on the building's second story. The detainee is seated on a chair too low for an adult; its seat curved upward and at times is flat and perforated so that the hole-rims etch themselves in the flesh of the person sitting on them; he is unable to move much, for his arms are constantly and snugly tied behind the back of the seat, also curved. In this state he is required to answer the questions of his interrogators, seated opposite him at a table with a computer and taking turns every few hours, each interrogator in his own shift. After many hours the detainee is taken down to his cell to sleep, and the next day he is brought up again to the interrogation room. However, some detainees are left in the interrogation rooms for days on end, nonstop. At times the interrogator asks the detainee questions, and sometimes he sits with his arms folded and remains silent, or reads a newspaper, or is busy with his computer like an office clerk. And sometimes he leaves the room—after blindfolding the shackled detainee—and disappears, for a short or long while, one never knows, for there is no clock and anyway the detainee's eyes are covered. And even without the blindfold the shut windows in these rooms do not reveal whether the sun is still shining or has already set, and perhaps it's already evening in the city when nearby streetlamps and office lights are on and ceiling lights and intimate table lamps illuminate the many restaurants and cafés in the neighborhood.

One of the two people who told her about their detention here spent fourteen days and nights in the interrogation room, and the interrogators managed to break him—he said this openly, with regret and shame. For fourteen days and nights he was there without seeing an attorney or anyone else except his interrogators, and from time to time a doctor who examined him and gave him pills of some sort, perhaps to ease the aches and discomfort caused by the difficult posture on the chair and the lack of sleep. He had to eat at the interrogator's table, and he was only allowed out of this room to use the toilet, and once a day to shower—perhaps for the convenience of the interrogators who spent time with him in such close quarters. After about four days and nights, he estimated, he nearly ceased answering questions and most of the time just sat on the little chair with his head bent, totally extinguished and apathetic.

When this part of his interrogation was over, he was taken down to one of the solitary confinement cells on the first floor. where he tried in vain to stop chilly air from blowing out of the air-conditioning unit by stifling it with an article of clothing, as his two blankets were insufficient. Perhaps also to silence its constant hum and try to get some sleep before being taken up to another day of interrogation, seated and tied to the little chair facing the ever-changing interrogators. At nighttime he would be returned to solitary confinement, sometimes this cell, sometimes that, time and again.

Several times he was brought in front of a military judge for remand, and beforehand he had to stand in the corridor like the ones who followed him and were seen by the woman, shackled and blindfolded and stuck against the wall or hidden behind a door. Finally he spent some days in a cell with three other detainees—perhaps they were supposed to get him to talk, he wasn't certain—until the fifty-seven days were over, at the end of which he was not tried but sent to one of the prisons for two years of administrative detention.

Not everyone undergoes such a long and arduous interrogation, said the two ex-detainees, not everyone is denied sleep for so many days at a time; some are not denied sleep at all. But the interrogation is always conducted in this manner: one is seated on one of the versions of that low chair, arms tied behind. And the solitary confinement cells are all dark and windowless and cold, and the sink and the latrine hole in the floor are filthy and crawling with mice.

## Mice

The mouse that sneaked out under the mysterious door in that military courtroom and the mice that fill the drain holes in the solitary confinement cells behind other doors were not at all as bad as the one mouse she actually killed with her own hands at home on the morning of one of those days she spent at the Russian Compound. The mouse she killed was one of the many mice that multiply from time to time in her apartment, running past her morning, noon, and evening, and at night they rustle in corners and leave their tiny black feces behind, and are not tempted to approach the morsel of cheese or sausage she leaves for them inside cages so they can live rather than die and she can set them free somewhere far from her home. Until, tiring of their presence, she sets small cubes of a certain greenish powder behind cabinets and toilet bowls and sinks, and these cubes do tempt them to take a bite, such is the power of that powder: they eat and then bleed slowly as the powder causes them internal hemorrhages, until they die. They die discreetly, for this too is the power of that powder, not killing the small rodents right away but rather injuring them so they suffocate gradually and urgently need to come out—to which end it is recommended to leave open the screens of windows and doors—and they will then die outdoors somewhere, unseen by eyes reluctant to witness their dying. And so they gradually disappear from her apartment, as if they are not dead at all but only freed into the neighbors' blossoming gardens.

One mouse, however, did not disappear this way. It must have already been ill and too exhausted to get out, and stood there one morning quite visible at the foot of the sofa. She came at it with a broom to chase it out or maybe kill it. But the little creature still found enough strength to run away from the broom underneath the sofa, and crouched in one of the corners, looking at the woman and her broom with its two tiny eyes, their living spark not yet extinguished, and saw her bend down on her knees and push the broom closer and closer until its brush enclosed it and hid the woman from the mouse and the mouse from the woman. Then the woman crushed the broom against the wall, pressed and pushed with all her might for many long moments, but when she finally pulled the broom toward her she realized the mouse was still curled up in its previous corner, not crushed but somehow seated on its behind, trembling. Then she got up and took a squeegee and once more got down and lay on her belly and struck the squeegee's hard rubber blade against the wall beneath the sofa, again and again and again, without looking at all, and at some point she let go and got up and took a deep breath, and when she bent down again, her whole body shaking, she saw the slight gray body lying in the corner on its side, its thin legs stretched forward. She crept toward it and stretched out her arm and collected it in the palm of her hand, and looked closely at this dead creature that just a moment earlier had brought out of her a violence that she hadn't known in herself—even spiders and other insects which she occasionally finds in her apartment she doesn't usually crush but rather hunts them carefully, holds them delicately in her fingers, and turns a small dish upside down over them, with a bit of newspaper underneath, and takes the captive insect outside to live rather than die.

## Epilogue

The detainees taken out of the detention facility in the heart of Jerusalem at the end of their interrogations may sometimes be seen for a moment as they are quickly loaded into vehicles on their way to prisons throughout the country, although passersby on Queen Helene Street are not likely to loiter at the gate and take a peek inside the yard. The metal arm blocking the entrance is usually not even down, and the entrance itself is very wide and the detention facility yard, even though surrounded by various walls and fences, can easily be seen from the lovely street, which has been renovated and renewed in recent years. If anyone did loiter there by chance or on purpose as detainees were loaded into a vehicle, he might see them blinking rapidly, their eyes no longer blindfolded. And perhaps he might notice the pale faces and limp bodies of some of them.

# CHILDREN

# Seeing Them See the Sea

This is the land. . . . I have caused thee to see it with
thine eyes, but thou shalt not go over thither.

DEUTERONOMY 34:4

"Ana bahib al-bahar," I love the sea, the girl said. They were
walking, stumbling along, on the sand, four children and one
grown woman. Backs, shoulders, and hands were laden with
backpacks and bags, the woman's hand and shoulder were
pulled down by the weight of a blue picnic cooler, and a red
sunshade protruded from under one of the children's arms.
Halfway, in the middle of all this discomfort, twelve-year-old
Nur stopped in her tracks and announced that she loved the
sea. "Ana bahib al-bahar," she said, and the other four who were
walking, stumbling, stood too and stared at her and then at
the sea, still a bit distant but lying before them, and Nur stood
motionless and gazed at it. The drive from her village to the
beach lasted no more than an hour and a quarter, but she had
never seen the sea before, nor had her eight-year-old brother
Mohammad, nor her cousins, ten-year-old Samir and seven-
year-old Yasmine. These vast marvelous expanses, the waves
breaking and foaming and disappearing and gently gathering to

the shore, the intense blue under the afternoon sun whose heat
was now receding, the breeze fluttering over arms and faces—
all this goodness and beauty were not meant for them or their
parents under the circumstances into which they were born.


The woman and the four children with her had crossed the
military checkpoint near the entrance to their village in her
red Ford Fiesta without stopping or being stopped. She had
no idea what the rules and regulations said in these parts: were
children, too, subject to the orders written on the large red
sign in front of the checkpoint, announcing that this crossing
is exclusively for Israelis? No, she really didn't know—perhaps
children were allowed even if they were not Israelis? There was a
rumor going around along those lines, she had even heard it in
the village, but she still felt her stomach contract and her knees
tremble as the car approached the soldiers' post. She feared
that the whole happy plan for this Friday would simply end,
vanish like a dream, after the children—and she too in fact—
had counted the minutes until it became real, so their parents
told her. Indeed, when she had arrived at the village they were
already waiting for her with their bundles at the foot of the steps
to their house, not the hint of a smile on their faces, stiff with
tension and uncertainty.

Yes, she too was nervous, afraid they would be stopped at
the checkpoint, instructed to pull over, asked questions, and
sent back. For a moment as they left the village, she thought
of telling the children not to speak Arabic until they passed
the checkpoint, as if they knew any other language. But they
didn't utter a word anyway, just sat there dumbstruck as she
slowly approached the military post, her stomach contracted

SEEING THEM SEE THE SEA

and her knees trembling, lowered her window, waved to the armed soldier, who signaled her to slow down even more and come to a full stop. She gave him a broad amicable smile and a nod, assuring him that both of them, he and she, belonged to the same side, to this nation, the lords of this land, all of which the soldier presumed anyway in view of the car and the face of its driver, and he returned her smile and greeting, and asked, "Everything all right?" to make sure her accent was the right one too, not just her looks. "Fine, great," she answered, but as he bent his head to get a look at the rest of the passengers through the car window, she stepped on the accelerator.

Come on, move, why pester me, let live, she said, or rather meant, and the soldier backed off to the side, was almost shoved back, and she drove on and gave a slanted look at the rear-view mirror and saw that he didn't care. *Ugh, who's got the patience for all these annoyances?* she thought. And into the silent space of the car she called out: "We're in Israel!" and surprised herself with the cozy feeling she had at the sight of all the greenery as they approached Mevo Beitar and Begin Park, in contrast to the mucky yellowish tone of the bare hills and ranges to the east. "We got across, we're in Israel! Going to the beach!"


All this was over. By now they had left checkpoint country far behind and even passed the pay booth at the entrance to Nitzanim Park, where no one wanted to check who and what they were, this woman and the quiet children with her, and simply received the entrance fees she paid. And she had found a space in the large car park at this beach, and all five of them had extricated themselves and their things from the car and begun to step silently across the sand toward the water.

It was then that Nur stopped in her tracks and declared: "Ana bahib al-bahar." And the woman looked at her and at the three other children who stopped as well, in different poses, as though playing Statues when the child who is It turns around to see who is moving and will be out of the game. But the woman was looking at the four of them in order to fully experience the moment, its richness and meaning, the moment she had looked forward to so eagerly since the trip was planned: to see them seeing the sea for the first time ever. Eyes wide open in surprise, beaming, lips slightly parted. A thread of saliva trickled from the corner of Yasmine's mouth—she was the youngest, and apparently she hadn't swallowed, Mohammad's large dark eyes grew almost round with wonder, Samir looked as though he was about to burst out laughing, while Nur, almost an adolescent, was serious, longing, dreamy, her eyes looking far off.

That moment probably grew very long only in the woman's own memory. In fact they must have hurried to find a spot among all the many people on the beach, the sunshades and chairs and mats and Styrofoam coolers and children and dogs and inflatable rings in all colors and sizes, among the sounds of portable radios and the clicks of wooden rackets hitting balls and shouts and talking in Hebrew and Russian and English, which would soon be mixed with the Arabic voices of Nur and Mohammad and Yasmine and Samir—for a little while they would still speak quietly among themselves so as not to stand out, but later they would forget and shout and yell at each other in these guttural tones that the elderly woman who accompanied them had such a hard time learning to pronounce correctly.

They fixed the red umbrella pole in the sand and spread a blanket in its shade. The woman told the children that here was their camp and they could put down their packs and bags and take off their shoes and go over to the changing stalls and change, and come back right away, and they must not go off without telling her and getting permission. They came back one by one, still obedient and disciplined. Nur now wore jeans and a T-shirt—she was only twelve and already obeyed the rules imposed on her gender in her society. Samir returned wearing bermuda shorts down to his knees, under which, when he finally began to scamper and skip around, a broad stripe of dark red underpants showed at his hips, giving him a rather fashionable look. Only Mohammad and Yasmine came back in bathing apparel—he in short phosphorescent green bathing trunks and she in a yellow-green bathing suit decorated with a kind of yellow skirt so short that it could by no means be regarded as concealing anything, perhaps quite the contrary: a mischievous provocation meant to reveal rather than conceal, to display the cute body of a healthy little girl, still retaining some of its baby fat.

This detailed description is being written from memory based on the hasty notes she took soon after the trip, that is to say a long time ago—Nur has married since then and is about to conclude her university chemistry studies, Samir dropped out of school and is working at a garage as a mechanic's apprentice, Mohammad is a high school senior and has grown up considerably since he appointed himself full caregiver to his elder brother, who was seriously injured in a traffic accident, and Yasmine has grown into adolescence and is not seen out of the house with her head uncovered. Now that the woman realizes her memory has retained so many details, she wonders why she

watched them so intensely back then, so precisely that their
movements and speech and clothing have been preserved in her
mind. She has no doubt that aside from being curious as to how
their parents equipped them to spend their first trip ever to the
beach, that careful gaze of hers had a practical purpose: to etch
in her mind the appearance of every one of them and remember
special marks so that she wouldn't lose them, God forbid. So
that if they suddenly discovered their freedom in these expanses
of sand and sea and get separated and distant and ran off each
in a different direction, she would be able to catch them at
least with her eyes, if not actually with her hands, which really
wished at the time to hold them on a leash somehow in order
to keep her promise to their parents to bring them back home
that evening safe and sound. She had made them this promise
without being asked, and they assured her they were not at all
worried. "Why worry? After all, the children are in your hands,"
Nur's father said and spread his own hands a little and then
placed his right hand over his heart, and they knew they could
rely on her as if she were their own mother. What nonsense, she
thought—when had she ever had four children to look after at
the beach, and what's more, children who didn't swim?

In the hours that followed, her careful gaze indeed helped
her search and find them: the jeans and blue shirt on Nur's
slim body, standing out of course among the bare girls on the
beach, and Yasmine's very short yellow skirt, and the red strip
of Samir's red underpants, and Mohammad's phosphorescent
green bathing trunks, he who was the one to disappear from
her view several times, as he was no different from several other
children in green bathing trunks. One, two, three, four, she
repeatedly counted them at first, one, two, three, four . . . No,
just three, where's Mohammad? "Mohammad's running over

there": Nur pointed. One, two, three, four . . . No, that's not Samir, where's Samir? "There's Samir, buried in the sand," Yasmine showed her.

But she also recalls, she remembers and knows that not just curiosity not just some practical motive caused her to observe so carefully and to let her gaze linger over the four children. It was a yearning, a desire to see these children as normal children, whose smooth skin was shiny with sea water, children whose ice cream mixed with sand was getting smeared over their flushed faces by the kiosk, simply children at the beach. For at home, in their village—where they are also simply normal children, in fact—she practically never saw them this way. From her point of view they were first of all part and parcel of that warped and distorted reality of a place fenced in with barbed wire and military jeeps driving to and fro along its main street, a place where armed soldiers often stop children on their way home from school to see if their hands show traces of hurled stones.

On that Friday they soon mixed in with other children at the Nitzanim beach, throwing sand and shells with them at the jellyfish that drifted to the shore to die without arousing anyone's compassion, and throwing sand and splashing water at each other, and then rolling down the sand dunes. And then their ice cream and popsicles got smeared all over their faces, and then the small group scattered and dispersed again and again. They really discovered their freedom, each in their own way.

She found Yasmine sitting on the sand and decorating with seashells a little sand castle she had built. She saw Samir, a short and sturdy boy, lying on his side, feet in the shallow water, head leaning on his elbow, quietly looking at the wet sand for a long time. She watched Nur from behind, standing at the water line, perhaps a yearning, dreamy look on her face again, her eyes gazing into the distance, longing for the promise of something new, exciting. And her eyes caught Mohammad as he ran over the flat rocks in the water, ran and bent and looked down and picked something out of the sea. She approached him and saw a little fluttering fish at his feet, and he picked it up and the fish fluttered in his hand.

"Put it right back in the water or it'll die. Hurry! Back in!" she yelled at him angrily, suddenly becoming hysterical. And the child was frightened and finally threw his meager prey back in the water. She peeped for a moment at the place where the fish dived among the rocks, and didn't dare check whether it was back in its own habitat to live or to die.


"See, I brought you all of them back alive and well," she told the many family members who gathered immediately around the red Ford Fiesta, out of which the four children quickly scattered and vanished, while she lingered in it for another moment to calm down a bit from the effort of driving to the sound of the children's songs and chants and clapping that had filled the car on the way back—how much more convenient had been the silence that filled the car when they drove in the other direction. Then she moved and pushed and lifted her behind from the driver's seat and got out a bit heavily, no longer nimble. *Why not exchange this car for a higher one?* she thought before she turned proudly to everyone around her: "See, alive and well."

Night had already fallen, darkness was upon the land beyond the checkpoint when they got back. No soldier stood there checking passengers in this direction, from Israel into the

West Bank, her stomach didn't flinch, her knees didn't quiver. Only her mind nearly burst from all the tension that had left her now, back safely with all four children—none of them had gotten lost, none had drowned. But unlike her, apparently none of their family members had feared for their safe return. It was not relief but radiance she saw; the many faces in the yard of that village home were actually radiant in the bright light of its lamp.

"You have no idea what an important thing you did," the father of Samir and Yasmine told her in Hebrew, and turned to deliver a short speech about how important it was to show these children that they could be among Jewish children, and look like them and play like them, how important it was that they grow up not just to hate. Besides, she had made their dream come true, seeing the sea, "and they won't ever forget this, they'll never forget you did this for them. Thank you, a thousand thanks."

She has a hard time reading these words now. Why? Are they naive? pathetic? Perhaps at that time they expressed a sincere, real hope, which since then has abandoned her heart as well as the heart of that speaker, he who is now a grandfather to children who are still forbidden to go to the beach, one hour's drive from their village.

# The Wonders
# of Ice Cream and What
# She Got Out of Them

It's a searing hot day in July. 38 degrees centigrade. At the entrance to the yard of the family home, a group of men and
children—just boys, no girls—sit at the doorway of a small
grocery shop, all holding ice cream cones. They're all licking ice
cream. White ice cream which in some of the lickers' cones still
shows the remains of a chocolate coating. The woman in the
red Ford Fiesta stops, lowers her window, and waves at them.
One boy gets up and runs toward her; he tells her that water is
dripping out of her engine. The father of the family and a few
other lickers take the trouble to get up and approach her, and
drops of melted ice cream trickle from the cones they hold and
seem to join the liquid dripping from the car to the ground. A
whole lump of ice cream loosens itself from the father's cone,
and she is sorry for this loss since at that moment she too yearns
to lick that ice cream; at home she would no doubt bend down
and pick up the ice cream from the floor and eat it. But she is
not offered a lick; they only check the drip from the car as she

sits inside, and one of the older children tells her, proud as a mechanic, that she has nothing to worry about, it's from the air-conditioning unit. Then she turns the key in the ignition, takes a sharp curve to the left, and carefully enters between the two wings of the iron gate in order to park her car inside the yard, where, in various shaded places, sit little girls licking ice cream too, and their red-and-white tongues loll out of their little faces smeared with vanilla-chocolate.

She gets out of the air-conditioned car into the shocking heat outside and climbs the familiar steps, entering the familiar living room—it's hot in there too—and jokes with the mother of the family about the crowd of ice-cream lickers outside, but the mother and her elder daughters offer her the usual juice that is too sweet and then coffee that is too hot and then tea that is too hot. No ice-cream cone is passed to the hand she holds out from her seat on the sofa toward one baby girl standing at her feet, to stroke her.

"It's not what you think, this ice cream," the father of the family begins a conversation with her having entered the living room a moment later. "It's not what you people eat. How much does ice cream cost you? Five shekels, maybe? Here it costs one shekel."

And surprised that he mentions this immediately, as if seeing right into her mind, she feels there's some matter here that bothers him a bit too, and asks: "And what's this one-shekel ice cream like?" He shakes his head and twists his mouth into a telling grimace.

"Nothing to write home about, eh?" she says. "Not at all," he answers, and now somewhere at the back of her mind she realizes he wished to let her know why she was not offered some of that ice cream, that was why he hurriedly followed her inside, but perhaps this dreadful heat makes her ignore this realization and speak in detail about the wonders of ice cream in her own world.

First of all, he wouldn't find any ice cream worthy of that name for five shekels; second, near her home is a special ice-cream parlor where fresh Italian ice cream is prepared every day, with flavors and aromas imported straight from Italy, and one scoop of such ice cream costs ten shekels, but can one make do with a single scoop when the stainless steel tubs behind the transparent plastic screen over the refrigerated counters are heaped with about twenty different mounds of ice cream, each flavor and color different from all the others? And third, at the beach to which she drove with the children a week earlier an ice-cream cone cost ten shekels, and an ice-cream bar coated with chocolate cost thirteen shekels—such are the prices in her world, neither one shekel nor five.

He listens to her, and after showing some interest in the quality of these expensive kinds of ice cream he repeats his familiar saying—that they, namely he and she, live in two worlds so different from one another—and adds: "Thank you, a thousand thanks!" for the pricy ice cream she bought the children back then and for the entire trip, and only then does she realize where this silly conversation has led and is very embarrassed. But the father of the family has already dropped the thanksgiving and begins telling her about the conversations the children have been having all week long—they've already given him a headache with all that talk about their time at the beach! The children who didn't go to the beach asked the children who did, how come they were not afraid to go to a place that was exclusively Jewish, with just *yahud*? Okay, the fact that they traveled with her, the woman they already know—that they could understand, there's one good Jewish woman, and that's her. But all the other Jews? And the children who went to the beach told the children who didn't that they saw lots of children at the beach, all of them in bathing suits, women and girls too, and not a single soldier and not a single army jeep—two of which had passed the woman on the main street of the village on her way here, dark and closed and barred, with all kinds of wires and antennas sticking up from their roofs—and those Jews there at the beach were good people, busy with their families and children, no one looked at the Palestinian children or pestered them. They were at ease there, even more than here when on an outing with their family in the village or its surroundings. In fact here they are not ever quite at ease.

"Because here," Nur later explained, having been on that trip to the beach and now coming to join them in the living room, "here when we go out to public places, everyone checks out everyone else, everyone looks at everyone, checking how a person and his wife and kids are dressed and how they behave, and in your parts they don't. To each his own, *lehalo*, everyone to himself, naturally, *bishakel tabi'i . . ."*

From here on the conversation proceeded to the differences between the two societies, to the adults' good memories of bygone years when they used to travel to cities and parks and the beach in Israel, and in these memories—the old memories of the adults and the fresh memories of the children—Israelis sounded like good people, an open and tolerant society, much more so than the Arab one. The woman sat and listened and didn't say anything; she had nothing to say this time.

Unlike one of her previous visits, when she did have something to say: she had exploded when one of the girls spoke of the humiliation she had experienced crossing one of the checkpoints, she and her mother were shoved back, or they were yelled at to get lost, or both—whatever—and throughout she called the soldiers *yahud*. And she, their guest, interrupted her at some point and asked her to please say soldiers, not *yahud*, and even found herself adding: "I'm Jewish too, see." The girl blushed and apologized and explained at length that until she had met the woman she had never seen Jews except for those soldiers, so they were the only Jews in her eyes and in her life, but now that she'd met her it was different, of course.

The speaker got entangled and was not frank, and the guest does not recall how they finally got out of this complication, these good Arab women and this good Jewish woman. Perhaps the hostesses offered her more coffee or cake, or juice or tea, which automatically resulted in the chain of thanks and niceties they exchanged, something like *shukran* (thanks) and *yislam ideiki* (bless your hands)— *'afouan* (you're welcome), *wideiki* (bless your own hands), *sahtein* (enjoy).

# A Beauty Spot, a Pearl

"This is the land. . . . I have caused thee to see it with thine eyes, but thou shalt not go over thither." This verse actually crossed her mind many times as she gazed out from the heights of the village of Batir over the beautiful valley below, the houses of Walaja village down the hill slopes on the other side, the old railway winding below, and the slopes on this side, where, invisible to them, is a gem of a place for children as well as for the adults accompanying them: the Jerusalem Biblical Zoo.

They shall not go over thither, neither the children of Batir, nor those of Hussan nor of Nahalin nor of Wadi Fuqin, the four villages so close to the valley where the railway is the border that their inhabitants must not cross, not even approach. Their farmlands on both sides of the railway have been confiscated as well—this is an ugly affair whose consequences are immense in the lives of people in these villages, thousands of families for generations.

But the woman has a much more modest tale to tell here, of one thrilling visit to the Biblical Zoo, conceived and carried out in the heart of the strange geographical, political, and human reality that has emerged here, an absurd man-made collage in the midst of creation.

The Biblical Zoo is very close to the family homes of the four children—the same four who drove with her to the beach—closer to them than even to her own Jerusalem home. Thus every time she went to visit the families and circled the roundabout below Malha, from which another road leads to the zoo and yet another turns in the direction of "Etzyon Bloc via Walaja," she was gripped by a wish ending with a question mark: why not dare just once to take the children to the zoo?

Days went by, weeks and months, and it became less easy to get to "Etzyon Bloc via Walaja." Things in this region are in constant flux. Here one bright day, before the checkpoint at the beginning of the beautiful road climbing along the valley, the Walaja Checkpoint—or En Yael Checkpoint in Hebrew, now titled "crossing" and neighboring new prestigious, spacious, and fancy reception premises—all of a sudden a large red sign stood, saying: "No way through to Etzyon Bloc via Walaja."

When she first saw the sign, she turned back and took the Tunnel Road, a boring, even ugly route. Therefore on her next trip she decided to check it out: how come there's no way through? After all the road does go up to Walaja and continues to Beit Jala, and in front of the Beit Jala checkpoint—no Jews allowed, only Arabs—there is a right turn to a road descending across the Talitha Kumi School directly to the junction on Road 60, where one can turn left and continue south to the Etzyon Bloc as well as to the Arab villages, many of which are not even named on the road signs, and to the large settlements of the Etzyon settlement bloc, all of them marked very clearly. So why all of a sudden is access impossible from there to the settlements?

Well, she did drive along that road. After Beit Jala there was another red sign, identical to the previous one, insisting again that the road to the Etzyon Bloc was closed. She ignored it as well and drove on. But down the hill she realized the two signs had not lied: the junction of that road with Road 60 was now marked clearly with signs and arrows indicating that no left turn, only a right turn, was allowed. In other words back to Jerusalem through the giant, multiple-lane checkpoint which at that time was still under construction that lacerated the landscape in every direction, until the wounds had become scars of a tall concrete wall curving generously and tilted at amazing angles—an architectural feat arousing awe and wonder when seen from above and claustrophobia when seen from below—and this checkpoint too was paradoxically titled a "crossing." At any rate, the left turn was now forbidden, so Palestinian passengers traveling from Beit Jala had to end their ride here at this junction: they must turn back.

Unless, of course, they held Israeli IDs, for then they could do what she did that time and continued doing on other occasions, although it was neither convenient nor safe: turn right instead of left, push her way rudely through the lanes at the checkpoint where cars—mostly from the settlements—crowded in waiting lines, bumper to bumper, on their way to Jerusalem, push through and get to the lane farthest to the left, thrust the red bumper of her Ford Fiesta into line, cross the checkpoint in this lane, courtesy of the private security firm and the soldiers in charge, and then immediately make a dangerous U-turn to the left.

That's it. Now she could drive another few hundred meters and turn right at the sign saying Beitar Ilit and Tzur Hadassah and Beit Shemesh, and drive to Batir and Hussan and Nahalin, whose names did not appear on it, or proceed to Efrata and Neve Daniel and Alon Shevut and even reach Kiryat Arba (all

settlements). And if one wished—why would one wish it if this
weren't a must?—one could also take a peek along the way at
Al Aroub refugee camp, crowded among tall barbed-wire fences
at the side of the road, and at the villages of Beit Umar and
Bani Naim, and other Arab localities of whose existence Israelis
traveling this road are not even aware, while those travelers who
do know, and perhaps even have relatives or friends there, don't
usually own cars, and even if they do, they had better not drive
them, for exorbitant fines are most diligently imposed on Palestinian drivers on this road. More than once she witnessed this,
while she herself was never required to pay such steep fines for
committing precisely the same traffic violations. And therefore
on second thought, there was perhaps some logic to the fact
that the names of these localities did not appear on the signs.

So she checked and found out on that occasion that she
could go on driving to the village along the scenic Walaja road
that overlooks the site of the zoo hidden between the hills to
the right of the road, nearly invisible, although in the meantime
below it, not invisible at all, a national park has emerged with
trails and car parks and nice recreation areas and even a special
bicycle track paved for cyclists like herself, while to the left of
the road a high wall has been erected, separating the park and
all of Jerusalem from Walaja village, both the ancient ruined
village and the newer one, on whose lands the park was built.


Days passed again, and months, the four children—Nur,
Samir, Mohammad and Yasmine—were now a year older, it
was summer vacation time, and a day was finally picked for the
trip to the zoo: Tuesday. The woman suggested it, remembering
the traditional belief that Tuesday, on which God said twice

that it was good, is the luckiest of days, and her heart told her that perhaps on this day they would be better protected from the dangers en route. It was superstitious, but sometimes she definitely needed superstitions. Especially when she was apprehensive, for then she was rather apprehensive of the dangers, even fearful—a woman on her own traveling time and again in a hostile reality, hostile and constantly changing for the worse.

That Tuesday, on her way to the village via the Walaja road, she slowed down as she crossed En Yael checkpoint, looking at the faces of the soldiers and trying to figure them out: were they nice? not so nice? It was hard to tell—they seemed a bit heat-struck. But what worried her was the scant number of cars passing through, perhaps thwarted by the red sign announcing the road no longer led to the Etzyon Bloc, so the soldiers had ample time to check every single car, and perhaps they even felt like doing so, out of sheer boredom.

And so all along the way she deliberated how to drive the children to the zoo: take this direct route, so short, or extend the trip and choose the Tunnel Road, where the checkpoint is usually very busy so inspection is much faster. Either way she would have to ask Nur to remove her hijab, which by that time—a sign that she had menstruated—she had learned to wrap skillfully around her head in perfect color schemes. Nur, who seemed so grown up, had better have her birth certificate on hand to prove she was still a minor and didn't need a permit yet, because this the woman had learned by now: Palestinian minors do not need permits.

But she also learned this: at neither checkpoint is a Palestinian, whether young or old, allowed passage. Palestinians have other checkpoints where they can either cross or be blocked, checkpoints where no Israeli, whether young or old, is allowed to pass. In other words, she and they must not pass together. All of this she had learned—checkpoint rules are a science, she told herself, and I need to master them especially well if I have decided not to give a damn about them.

Either way, on that Tuesday by the time she had arrived at the village she was still unable to choose between the shorter Walaja road and the longer Tunnel Road, between the two checkpoints. She kept shifting her choice from one to the other. And at the doorway of the family home, while the children crowded into the Fiesta and bickered over the window seats, she hesitantly asked the father and the uncle for their opinion: should she cross the Walaja checkpoint or the Tunnel Road checkpoint? She felt slightly ashamed for asking, but the father—who, not daring to give her instructions unless she asked for them, but very much waiting for this question—replied immediately: take the Tunnel Road, it's just ten minutes more, no big deal. And they took off.


On the way, as she passed by the turnoff to Walaja, she still hesitated. The right turn up the road is allowed, unlike the left turn downhill, and the road was open for a fast drive, just a quarter of an hour to the zoo. But she proceeded to the checkpoint waiting lines, careful to choose the lane for Jewish Israelis and to be just like them, like the settlers who make up the majority of the people crossing here, and perhaps among them some were taking their children to the Biblical Zoo too, for this was summer vacation; even the religious had time off their yeshiva studies.

She had to slow down only a little as she passed the woman guard, armed and wearing a bulletproof vest, and then a soldier;

both nodded, signaling that she could proceed. But after only a few meters a loud shout sounded behind her: "Back up!" and she slammed on the brakes. Oh no, how scared she was, this cowardly woman—no, rather worried than scared—who so far had not had a single contented moment on this zoo trip, certainly wasn't calm and relaxed, not even when she glanced at the rear-view mirror and saw that neither the guard nor the soldier was looking at her; their faces were turned to other cars, coming from the south, so the shout was not meant for her. She then accelerated and continued driving, and nothing happened.

They entered the first tunnel. "Look," she cried, feigning merriment the way adults do to children on a trip: "Look, a tunnel, and it's very long, you're seeing it for the first time, right?"

"Right," a child's voice answered from the rear, not at all merry, still scared and tense. And she too was now gripped by a new fear because the tunnel suddenly grew dark, as it always did at this particular spot that for some reason is not adequately illuminated, and she realized that once more she had forgotten to change her sunglasses for her usual ones, that she was driving too fast, much too fast, and needed to calm down, take control, slow down—slow everything down, her thoughts and ideas as well as her movements and speech. *Slow down*, she told herself, *easy does it, you'll end up having an accident and then the children will not get back safe and sound, and not because of any checkpoints or soldiers.*


She was so eager to slow down, let go, relax, that after they arrived at the zoo and entered its gates and along with their tickets picked up a map of the zoo—a map in Arabic for each child, for in this zoo the information for visitors is written in both Hebrew and Arabic, and that was another reason she had been eager to bring the children here—she sat the four children down. Now they were finally showing the normal gaiety of children and were excited about the good time they were about to have there, and their eyes were wandering with amazement across the pond at the entrance, a watery surface in the midst of lawns and trees and well-tended greenery and black and white ducks and swans floating across, with an island in the middle and large monkeys swinging on ropes and hammocks tied to many tree branches. But she seated them and herself on the lawn and announced that they had plenty of time, lots and lots of time and no reason to hurry, and in order to get the most from their visit, they should first carefully study the map and decide what they wanted to see and in what order.

She herself leaned back on her forearms, making herself comfortable in a semi-reclining position and prepared to take in the full pleasure of this shady pause in body and mind, luxuriate in this fresh green garden, which now she actually regarded as the promised land: this is the land, I have let thee see it with thine eyes, and thou shalt go over thither.

This pause did not last long, though, as the children were not seeking any promised land but simply looking for a zoo, and the freedom to move and run around and maybe even horse around. Their look at the map was reluctant—why should they be glad about a text written in Arabic in the land of the Jews? Perhaps they even forgot they were in the land of the Jews, not promised to them! They began demanding to get on: why don't we go? No, she answered, take a look first and decide what you want to see. But Samir got up and approached her and showed her the pavilion of little animals on the map, then pointed to the pavilion nearby: it was right there beside them, so why not go there immediately? and what's the use of a map here—they can see it!

And they all got up at once and ran and vanished inside the little animals' pavilion, and then rushed on to the parrots' large cages, and stopped on the way to look at penguins, and asked when they would finally get to see the lions and elephants, and this was the end of the political-humanist act that she had had in mind which by now had turned into an outing of something resembling a family with plenty of children, one of those Jewish ultra-Orthodox families and the few secular families who filled the zoo on this summer vacation day. And she became a kind of untimely mother, perhaps grandmother, and almost as she had done at the beach, she counted them again and again to make sure all four were with her, and bought popsicles and gave out wafers and shouted at them a little and laughed a little, and finally—at the end of four exhausting hours—found herself pleading with them to come away from the playground filled with swings and ladders and nets and lovely painted sculptures covered with shiny mosaic, and urging them to leave and get back to the car—and home.

She had already given in to their pleas to stay once before, when she hadn't had the heart to take eight-year-old Yasmine off the swing, which she had finally gotten to use because a little girl in a pink buttoned-up dress and white knee socks gave it up for her. This little girl's father, with side curls and a black skullcap, had urged her a little while earlier to sit beside Yasmine— she told this to her mother later in the village—and play with her, and Yasmine drew a very large heart in the yellowish sand. How could one find the right words for such kitsch, and for such sticky emotions?

There were other special moments in this abnormal normality of the trip to the zoo, moments made for them by some zoo employees. For instance, one guide upon hearing that the children came from the West Bank, accompanied them for a long while with explanations in Arabic although she wasn't really fluent except with the names of the animals, but she knew just how to be friendly with children. And there were animal feeders who let the children enter one of the pavilions even though it was about to be closed to the public because it was feeding time. All the workers needed to hear was that these children could not come easily to the zoo.

"From the West Bank, near the Etzyon Bloc?" they asked. "So what? Can't they come here with their parents? Why not come here with their schools? So many Arabs visit here."

"Because there are checkpoints and restrictions and military rule," she responded. "What, haven't you heard?"

"No, we don't go there, into the Territories. Good for you, bringing them here."

"But it's very simple," she said lightheadedly, and in one short utterance made all her fears and deliberations disappear. Perhaps they had really been exaggerated—that's how they seemed to her now.

"If it's simple," they said, "maybe we'll do it too."

"Sure, do it!"

And in the meantime—until these young zoo workers themselves could begin smuggling children from the West Bank to the zoo—they allowed the four children to watch the big elephants while they ate and their pen was closed to visitors, and to pet the little animals at the petting corner while other children clung to the closed gate because here too it was feeding time and the corner was closed to the general public and open only to Nur and Mohammad and Samir and Yasmine. After a while the four went out among the clusters of those pleading in vain to get in, and the gate closed behind them—behind, not in front of them!

In front of them lay the colorful playground, where Yasmine drew the big heart after getting off the swing.

# THE SEASONS IN HEBRON

# Autumn: Through the Hole That Once Was a Lock

*Israel then shall dwell in safety alone*
*(Deuteronomy 33:28)*[1]

A little Jewish boy runs down the street alone. His hair is blond and curly, his snow-white festive shirt as well as the fringes of his *talith* (ritual undergarment) blown by the wind. He runs toward a neat asphalt circle shaded by palm trees at a large junction at the bottom of the hill, where two road signs with circles of arrows indicate a traffic roundabout. But the child who keeps running down the middle of the street seems to know that no vehicles are on the move here today in the Old City of Hebron, for this is a Jewish holiday, Simhat Torah. The

---

1. The titles of the sections here are quotations from *parashat vezot habracha*, the portion of the Torah read in Simhat Torah—a Jewish holiday that celebrates and marks the conclusion of the annual cycle of public Torah readings, and the beginning of a new cycle.

woman's eye follows the back of the little runner, who now trots merrily past a huge poster placed at the side of the junction to welcome visitors—those who have probably arrived already and those still expected—with a warm holiday greeting, and past the single soldier standing guard in safety in the middle of this vast empty area, only a small skullcap covering his head. The eye also sees the soldier smile at the boy and the boy disappear in the distance, and then the eye returns to the sloping street that now, without the boy, is entirely deserted.

### *This is the land which I sware unto Abraham, unto Isaac, and unto Jacob (Deuteronomy 34:4)*

All the shops on the right side of the street are shut behind light blue iron gates shaded by curved metal awnings, also painted light blue, all apparently made to match. On these awnings, all seemingly daubed with the same paintbrush, even the light orange-brown rust stains echo each other, and the woman's attentive eye—she is here on a visit—responds to them and is drawn up the street, until it lingers a little on the two torn flags of the State of the Israel, proudly set atop a streetlamp that is cleverly designed to look like a gas lamp of bygone days. But no, closer up the eye sees that only one of the two flags is in fact that of the State of Israel, while the other is unfamiliar to her. It's also not certain that the flags are torn; perhaps the wind has just curled them around their poles and onto the wires and ropes dangling from the barred window above them, which now catches her eye. This window has two grids, one dirty white with large squares, and the other, behind it, brown, perhaps rusty, its squares small and dense. Beyond the two grids it's hard to make out the dark panel that covers this already tightly secured window. Is it a wooden shutter? an iron one? There are certainly no glass panes nor curtains, not in this window nor in the ones in the houses up the street, all barred and shut.

Suddenly, when the woman's eye has grown accustomed to following the upward slope of the street with its geometry of dark squares under the roofs of the low houses, it runs into a violent large black mark on the ashlar stone wall of one of the houses. It looks like soot, spreading not above windows but rather above three matching arched doors, also barred and shut, that open—or rather close—onto a small balcony. And the eye imagines the fiery tongues that burst out of these doors trying perhaps to destroy the house, which is probably empty of its inhabitants by now. But maybe not—perhaps people do live there, who knows, just as in the other houses there's no way of knowing whether the barred and shut windows protect any current inhabitants. At any rate, the flames that may have aimed to destroy this house were quickly extinguished, so it seems, because closer up the woman's eye sees that what the fire had time to devour before it was put out was nothing but a large bush that grew and perhaps bloomed among the stones, and now in the air and against the wall its thin charred branches form dense black lace contrasting with a sheet of white plastic trapped in it, as though echoing the white in the flags seen earlier, both sheet and flags almost spotless, although clearly no one here bothers to keep them respectable and pristine. Below the lace and the porch, the eye catches another tiny white echo upon a rust-brown awning, and needs to move very close to it, perhaps even use field glasses, and then realizes it's a sticker that someone bothered to climb and paste up there: "Na nach na-

chm nachman me-Uman" (a Hasidic Jewish mantra honoring
Rabbi Nachman of Bratzlav, buried in Uman).

*O people saved by the Lord, the shield of thy help, and
who is the sword of thy excellency!* (*Deuteronomy* 33:28)

The eye of the woman touring this street tires of its careful
study of these sights and wishes to roam more freely the vast
blue sky above. And lo, even there in the bright heaven it is
caught by a dark line against the background of white cumulus
cloud, which then turns out to be not a line in the cloud but
rather a person standing alone on a rooftop. He wears a broad-
brimmed hat and carries a large rucksack, his profile smiling at
the horizon. One might think his gaze too is roaming the sky or
the rooftops. But closer still he turns out to be an armed soldier
stuck on the roof between two concrete blocks. The soldier
looks down at the street, and she too lowers her gaze, slowly
following the barrel of his cocked rifle and finally lingering on
the house wall from which various wires stretch and lead to
small squares in a large empty metal frame. These are electrical
wires, and the frame must have contained a shop or workshop
sign that used to be lit up in the evenings by power supplied
through these wires. Since the frame is now empty, there's no
knowing what trade or crafts person used the space closed behind the blue metal shutter below. Well, one could know if
one insisted—this the eye suddenly discovers: a medium-sized
black square board hangs above the missing sign and on it the
word *khatat* is written in simple letters in white oil paint, meaning a sign painter worked here, perhaps a designer, certainly
someone skilled in calligraphy. Eventually, as the deserted street
does not offer the eye a human shape on the ground, the eye is

now attracted to the small signs over the shops, which seem to proliferate as the eye insists on looking more intently.

## *The fountain of Jacob* shall be *upon a land of corn and wine (Deuteronomy 33:28)*

*Sisan a'alaf mu'adat muza* is written on one of the signs, and together the chicken drawn beside the words and the woman's pocket dictionary help her determine that someone must have once traded here in poultry and chicks, animal feed and farm equipment. The telephone number provided below might enable her to find out where they are now, this shopkeeper or keepers, how they are and what they do: 052387811. Only nine digits, so it's not a working number now that a tenth digit has been added to all phone numbers. Perhaps the cell phone company could supply the missing digit.

But she will not inquire. It's not the shopkeepers—now it's the poor chicks she feels sorry for: the myriad soft, downy chicks that she imagines as she continues up the main street of the Old City of Hebron and realizes that many of the signs over closed shops here include the word *sisan*. She envisions them caged, convulsing, suffocating in that horrific crush, and in a moment she might even hear their tweeting in the silent street while she idly repeats this hissing word, *ssssissssan*. It's the harsh half-guttural Arabic *s*, not the frontal hiss *ss*, she reminds herself as she places the tip of her tongue against the bottom of her front teeth and tries in vain to produce the right sound from the depth of her mouth cavity. And quits. And proceeds up the ghostly street and makes an effort to decipher the other words written on the signs she passes, informing her that beside chicks and other poultry, the fruits of the earth were once sold here, including fodder and other sorts of animal feed. One shop, according to its sign, sold animal products, eggs and meat, to feed the owners of livestock and their customers. This sign was rather more difficult to approach because of a barrier of concrete blocks closing off the side street on the corner where that shop stood—a barrier sporting graffiti that announces that "Markovitch was here and screwed girls"—and in front of the concrete blocks there are rolls of barbed-wire fencing, commonly called *taltalit*, "curly," put there by someone probably too lazy to cut it, so that a rather large roll was left behind that could protect the other barriers of barrels and concrete blocks that close off all the streets branching toward the right from Shuhada Street[2]— protect them from skilled climbers who might wish to cross from this side to the other, hidden side.

### *I have caused thee to see it with thine eyes, but thou shalt not go over thither (Deuteronomy 34:4)*

Indeed the eye too longed to cross at last from one side to the other, and to satisfy that longing, the woman walking on her own in the deserted Old City of Hebron found no other way but to deviate a bit, approach a small door set in the concrete blocks of one of these barriers, which happened not to be protected by any "curly," and try to open it. But the door would not open, although it had no lock, only an empty hole at approximately eye level, undoubtedly a hole into which a lock had once fitted, for this looked like someone's front door. But

2. Shuhada was the main street of the Palestinian Old City, a very lively street until the Jewish settlement was illegally built there. Today no Palestinian cars are allowed here, only Israeli.

through this hole in the door, to which the woman walking here alone in safety clung with her entire long body (which to her dismay had begun to thicken in recent years), no furnished rooms could be seen—in this area pieces of furniture appeared only lying among large piles of trash, and also on one shop sign she'd passed a moment earlier, in a drawing of a double bed surrounded by curtains and chests of drawers whose color had faded and would soon disappear too under the green creeper on the wall of that shop, decorating it with its blue blossoms. Through the round hole devoid of a lock she saw a little alley, quiet and pleasant-looking, with three people in it. Two of them, well dressed, seemed to be walking and talking at leisure as they passed under a stone arch to another little alley.

These two people gave the woman standing there on her own, safe and undisturbed, a surprising moment of joy. The whole scene, through the round hole, reminded her of others she had observed with great pleasure through the circle of a magnifying glass during her travels, scenes painted with the fine brushes of Flemish Renaissance painters. Only a magnifying glass, which she always carried when visiting art museums, reveals the details of an ancient urban landscape lying beyond the tall narrow windows of a room or through the openings of a manger in which a fat little baby lies on its back, its head crowned with a halo. Only a magnifying glass reveals the details of the beautiful arches over alleys and streets and the few passersby in them—who, like these two here, seem to be walking and talking at their leisure.

But in the foreground of the picture seen through that hole without a lock in the deserted Old City of Hebron there were no virgins or saints or kings, but rather a small bulldozer and a man sitting in its cabin. The bulldozer was still, made no noise, and did not disturb the picture, and therefore the eye at first ignored it and tried to reach deeper, beyond the arch and the two people underneath, as it had learned to do from those beloved paintings. The eye penetrated deeper and discovered that the alley where the two men were headed also had closed shops, and there too, just as on this side, the awnings were rusting.

### *Smite through the loins of them that rise against him, and of them that hate him, that they rise not again (Deuteronomy 33:11)*

Now that the eyes of the woman walking silently and alone had had their fill of the visible and hidden sights up Shuhada Street and the alleys branching off it—and perhaps she had had enough of walking on her own, and perhaps she feared that phantoms would appear—she began to make her way back down the street, striding more hurriedly, no more lingering, except in front of a large sign that read as follows:

> The ancient Jewish quarter purchased and built by the Hebron Jewish community was destroyed by the Arabs after the massacre of 1929, and destroyed again in 2007 by order of leftist elements and the legal system

But she did not have the time to delve into this sign's upsetting story and clarify the matter, for just then she was plucked out of her silent solitude by a merry procession of men in festive white shirts coming toward her. They sang and danced, holding Torah scrolls. And immediately a police van stopped next to her, and out of it came a police officer who asked who she was and where from, and said that this area had been declared a closed military zone and began to explain to her politely the whys and wherefores, as this place—surely you know—is sensitive both religiously and politically, and today only its inhabitants are allowed to be here. He pointed to Abed and Abu Abed, owners of souvenir shops on the other side of the street, standing idle in their shop doorways, and he also pointed to the celebrants who had now reached her and the police officer, and just then Baruch Marzel (an American-born Orthodox Jew living in the Jewish community of Hebron in Tel Rumeida) emerged from their ranks and ordered the officer to cease his idle talk with the unknown woman and remove a whole group of journalists and photographers who were pestering the procession and desecrating the sanctity of this holiday by working. And the officer hurriedly cut through the procession and approached the uninvited guests—who immediately disappeared, poof! Gone.

## *Epilogue*

The woman in light blue jeans and dark blue T-shirt carrying a small backpack, who at that moment was no longer on her own but now feared that she would no longer make her way in this place in safety, also hurried back to her red Ford Fiesta parked outside the Old City of Hebron, and drove home and looked at the photographs she had taken and wrote the story of the sights her eyes had seen in the Old City of Hebron on the day when thousands of Jews celebrated their Torah festival and the Arab inhabitants were under siege.

# Winter: Blessed Be He Who Does Wondrous Deeds

## *Prologue*

Blessed are You, Lord our God, King of the Universe,
Who formed man in wisdom
and created in him many holes and hollows.
It is revealed and known before the Throne of Your glory
that were one of them to be ruptured, or blocked,
it would be impossible to survive and to stand
before You even for one hour.
Blessed are You, Lord,
Healer of all flesh, who does wondrous deeds.

The woman in dark blue jeans and black woolen coat stood facing this inscription, written in large white letters on a black rectangular board fixed to a concrete wall in Hebron, and wondered. Her jaw must have dropped a bit, as it was wont to do in moments of pondering and wondering, and she was caught up in existential thoughts about holes and hollows and cavities, not necessarily in the body but in life in general, getting blocked and opened and blocked again, and sometimes blocked never to be opened again. Until she came to her senses and scolded herself, annoyed: *What is wrong with you, getting carried away like that? Better check whether you need to empty your own hollow before you go walking on your own in this deserted ghost town— this is just a latrine wall!* And indeed not only the beautifully stylized prayer on the wall but also the request beneath it, written on a transparent board implied exactly that: "Kindly keep this place clean." However, the full request—"Please, kindly keep this place clean as befits the heritage of the Patriarchs"— was still proof that this was not a wall of just any latrine but rather one in the facade of a holy site.

The woman in dark blue jeans and black woolen coat stood on that winter day at the foot of the fortified compound of the Cave of the Patriarchs in Hebron. She lingered there for a short while before going forth to walk about the town and confirm firsthand, and not for the first time, that just surviving for one hour or more in this place, in this town, in its ancient quarter, does reveal how the Healer of all flesh, and perhaps His inspiration for human beings, and perhaps the force of life and the desire to survive and continue to exist—and even to mock life—does wondrous deeds, although the actual deeds and incidents are rather strange at times, like those that happened to her as she moved away from that compound.

## *First Incident: An Embarrassing Encounter*

In a nearby alley something suddenly hit her head, cold and wet. She stopped and looked up, and something cold and wet landed on her again. This time it hit her face. Scandalous. She held it in her hand and took a closer look, and a little gray snowball melted in her open palm and dripped between her fingers. This was a meager remainder of snow that had fallen here recently; solid little piles of it were still to be seen here and there on the sides of the alley, no beauty or majesty to it. "Don't throw stones, you son-of-a-bitch!" someone screamed next to her. The accent was Mizrahi (here meaning Jewish Israeli of Arab cultural origins), the inflection very precise, in perfect Israeli military style. But the voice was too thin. She had to lower her gaze to find the face and mouth that produced it: a child with black hair, short in front and stuck to a light-complexioned forehead, black eyes shining underneath. His face was round, smooth, with puffy cheeks. Another filthy snowball crashed against the muddy soil at her feet. And again: "You heard me, you son-of-a-bitch! Don't throw stones!"

She moved away from the flying snowballs and turned to look at the child shouting next to her. "I'm not an Arab! I'm a Jew!" he shouted, this time to her. And again the intonation was perfect, but no longer army style, no longer commanding, instead defensive—in fact, rather like someone caught in the act of throwing stones and trying to put things right, first in a moderate voice and then with growing insistence, nervously, desperately, angrily: "I'm not an Arab! I'm a Jew!" he repeated again and again. The woman in dark blue jeans and black woolen coat carrying a small backpack gave him an astonished look, looked up seeking some explanation or perhaps help from the few passersby, some of whom had already come close and now stood next to her: two or three men, two women, observant Muslims judging by their head coverings and clothes, and several boys and girls. They stood and smiled. She and they already made up a small group, almost a gathering in the sleepy alley. She tried to make some kind of normal contact with the boy, as a grown woman does with children, looking at him with forced affection, uttered an incomplete phrase in halting Arabic, chuckled, held out a hand to stroke his hair, pat his cheek, but he withdrew and persisted. "Why are you speaking to me in Arabic?" he asked her in Hebrew, addressing her in the masculine in a cross, impatient voice. "We're Jews, not Arabs!" But his eyes were laughing now. There was rich laughter in those black shining eyes, provocative and teasing and amused, the eyes of a kid who has just pulled a mischievous trick. There was not a trace of alien accent in his voice: "I'm not an Arab. I'm a Jew." And he yelled again at the roof from which the snowballs had apparently been hurled. "You sons-of-bitches, throwing stones!" and the whole crowd around her laughed.

It was an embarrassing encounter. She hurried away.

## Second Incident: A Troubling Memory

"I'm Palestinian, you're not Palestinian!" a woman screeched, an observant Jew to judge by her head covering and clothes, at an Arab in a white shirt and dark jacket. "You people murder Jews because they're Jews. Jews have no right to live," she addressed the Arab, who in the meantime vanished from sight because the camera focused on that woman and her words.

The voice and words and that scene now clung to the memory of the secular Israeli woman in dark blue jeans and black woolen coat, who was still embarrassed but also slightly startled and anxious to get back to the well-protected plaza in front of the fortified compound of the Cave of the Patriarchs. The voice and words and scene were part of a video clip she had seen not long ago. The clip documented the Jewish residents of Tel Rumeida in Hebron chasing Arab harvesters away from a small olive grove.

It was a troubling memory. She shook herself out of it and took bigger strides.

### *Third Incident: An Upsetting Sight*

"The People of Israel Lives!" This slogan was written in large letters on a closed metal shutter of one of the shops, and the woman
in jeans and black woolen coat, who now walked rather fast,
slowed down again. The shutter was painted a dirty turquoise
blue, and the inscription, all across the shutter, was divided in
two: The top line read "The People of Israel" and underneath
"Lives!" between two slightly crooked Stars of David. Above the
shutter was an elegant symmetrical facade of a very old, perhaps
even ancient house. Its ashlar stone walls were still light of hue
and rather clean, and the ornaments intact: in the middle was
a rectangular oriel under a pediment, with an Arabic bas-relief
inscription inside a thin frame, and on either side of the oriel a
barred window and door, which in the past must have opened
onto a balcony; they were now closed to a concrete platform
without a banister. All of these were surrounded by quoins and
cornices and sculpted stones that made a rich assemblage of
geometric forms, angles, squares, and trapezoids. The protrud-
ing concrete platform, once a balcony perhaps, now shaded
the upper part of the inscription "The People of Israel," which
only darkened a bit but did not altogether disappear, whereas
the "Lives!" part and the two Stars of David, one brown like
the inscription and the other dark blue, were brightly lit by the
noon sun of that bright winter's day.

This was an annoying sight. She tore herself away nervously
and took even bigger strides.

### *Fourth and Main Incident: The Trip*

The woman in dark jeans and black woolen coat carrying a
small backpack returned to the well-guarded plaza in front of

the fortified compound of the Cave of the Patriarchs, and there for a while she watched a woman walking with a girl. She deliberated and then decided to follow them, and soon caught up with them and spoke to them. They were a mother and daughter, observant Muslims according to their dress, and the mother told her they were on their way home. Their home was very close, the mother said, but their way there was long and complicated; she could come along and see for herself. Yes, the woman wanted to come and see. That was exactly what she, the Israeli Jewish woman in jeans, wanted: to see for herself how the Arab inhabitants managed with the many holes and hollows that were blocked in their city by the Israeli Jews.

And she joined them. She with her head uncovered and they with theirs covered, she a tall woman, they short. It was especially their difference in height—which even her crooked gait did not erase—that bothered her as she walked alongside them, but just for a moment. Very soon, as they turned right from the plaza in front of the fortified compound of the Cave of the Patriarchs and entered the adjacent street, the three of them were dwarfed by the barrier blocking the street. This barrier was taller even than the Israeli Jewish woman, who as a child was nicknamed Giraffe and was frequently asked what the weather was like up there. Scandalous. So she ended up habitually hunching her back a little, straightening up only on very special occasions. For example, at the foot of that barrier in Hebron, where she stretched and straightened up to her full height—and not out of pride, for she was beside herself with shame. No, it was curiosity and the will to see all three barriers erected at differing heights one behind the other: the first, two large concrete cubes; behind it, tall rusty barrels standing next to and on top of each other, layer upon layer; and behind those two, a wall of metal plates welded together.

Their home stands on this street, the mother said, it's very near, but it's been a very long time since they could reach it from here, and she had brought her here only to show her—yes, she should see and know how they live here because of the Jews. She said this and turned back, with her daughter, and the Israeli Jewish woman turned back with both of them.

They entered another street and walked along it, and turned from it into another street and walked along that one, and then turned from that one into an uphill alley and walked up this alley as well, and then turned into a downhill alley and walked along it—and she with them, turning and walking uphill and down-hill. And lo, the farther they walked, the alleys looked cleaner, paved with large flagstones; one of the alleys even opened up into a small square with a well and a pulley for an old-fashioned bucket. And the walk already became a tour of a beautifully picturesque ancient town. Very quiet, too, for the alleys were nearly empty of people and the women were like vacationers, three women-vacationers strolling along in a small Italian town where, luckily, the hordes of tourists had evaporated.

However, they were not in a small town in Italy but in a restored quarter of the Old City of Arab Hebron; the Israeli Jewish woman in dark blue jeans was now seeing it for the first time. Wonder of wonders, she thought to herself, Healer of all flesh, and perhaps His inspiration, and perhaps simply the force of life and the desire of human beings to survive and continue to exist, did wondrous deeds here as well: a little while ago there was destruction and desolation, and right here was renewal— not fortresslike ghettos with huge stone buildings as in the re-built Jewish settlement in Hebron, in the midst of the ruined lives of others, but rather a restoration done in good taste—this the woman needs to state here very clearly and not at all as a matter of aesthetic judgment but rather as a declarative statement, and not a political but an architectural one. Even if made by a political woman who is no architect.

Yet all of a sudden without understanding how this came about—that woman never did have an outstanding sense of orientation—they were standing again at the foot of that three-layered barrier in the very same street from which they had begun their winding way just a while ago. But now they were on the other side of the barrier. She realized this not only because the mother invited her to enter their home right there but also because here the order was reversed: first the metal plate wall was seen in its entirety; then, from the steps leading up to the house, the tops of the barrels were seen behind it; and finally the concrete blocks were faintly visible beyond.

Wonder of wonders yet again: in the space between the metal plates and the pavement the heads of two children popped up at that very moment, and following the heads two thin and agile bodies squeezed into this side of the street, crawled a little farther on their bellies, and were then inside the small yard of the house. They got up right away and looked around them, victorious: they had not walked up and down alleys like their mother and sister but had squeezed between the concrete blocks, climbed the barrels, and slithered under the metal plates, and in a jiffy they were home. An obstacle course of sorts, a children's game, and perhaps training for future military skills—who knows, it does make sense somehow, doesn't it?

## *Epilogue*

The house was the home of one of the last families to remain at that time—winter 2008—inside this neighborhood at the heart of the Old City of Hebron, a neighborhood nearly empty of its inhabitants. The woman in dark blue jeans sat for a while in that family home; next to her, on the sofa, lay her black woolen coat, and at her feet, on the floor, the small backpack. She had a sweet orange drink and bitter black coffee, heard the father complain about life in the shadow of the checkpoints, and promised to look into several things for them and come back to visit them.

But she didn't go back—whether because she would never be able to find her way there on her own, or because she didn't make the inquiries that they needed. So she has no idea where they are now, the members of this family, and what has become of them. On the other hand, she has often stood in front of that sign and the prayer written on it, which one must recite when leaving the toilet. And her wonder and amazement never cease.

# Spring: Childhood

## *A Girl*

Opposite a residential building on a street corner in the Old City of Hebron, close to the plaza in front of the fortified compound of the Cave of the Patriarchs—where a mass of Israelis, men, women, and children, most of them religious Jews, were celebrating Passover that day—stood an Israeli police van. Three policemen stood next to it, maintaining peace and order.

Right then, as the three women were passing (the woman in jeans with her usual backpack was not alone this time: two other secular Israeli Jewish women were with her), someone upset the peace and order. Just below that residential building on the corner a man gave a five- or six-year-old girl a spanking. The girl cried and yelled, and the man—obviously her father, judging by the girl's shouts, and they were obviously Arabs, judging by the language she used—ordered her to get inside immediately. And there was another spanking and the girl disappeared inside the building and from view. The father's nerves were clearly frayed, perhaps because the girl had ventured out without permission into the very hostile world that closed in on their home just then.

Whatever the reason, the sobbing girl probably found solace in her mother's bosom, and the father probably meant to go about his business. But the Israeli policemen, stationed there for the welfare of the Jewish celebrants—thousands of whom continued swarming to the plaza—and perhaps protecting the few remaining Arab residents of the city from those same celebrants, witnessed the family scene. And since at that moment no Arab was harassing a Jew, nor was any Jew harassing an Arab, they felt obliged to concern themselves with the well-being of the Arab girl whose own father had harassed her—and if not with her well-being in particular, as she was already gone, then with that of the entire family, by educating the spanking father. Let this man learn a lesson in nonviolent family conduct. So they called him over, demanded to see his ID, looked it over, scolded him, and would not let him go on his way; no, they ordered him to go back to the house and return with the girl. They kept his ID.

The father obeyed, entered the house, and returned with the girl, her hand in his. Now the policemen instructed him on how to treat children—in front of his daughter's watchful eyes and open ears, perhaps so she too would learn her rights in twenty-first-century society. The father faced them, looking contrite and occasionally leaning down and hugging the girl, saying—to her or to the policemen—that he loved her.

This was all witnessed by the three women, she and her two friends who had come to watch Jews celebrating Passover in the Old City of Hebron. At this point they were more interested in the three policemen and the man and the girl who made up a strange cluster at the edge of the whirlpool of the celebrating crowd.

"Why did you take his ID, and what do you want with him?" one of them asked the policemen. The men stared, wondering, at the three women. One officer asked them if they hadn't seen how the father spanked the girl and didn't they know that it's against the law to spank children? In fact, he added, the law requires policemen to arrest the man, but this time, he said, they would make an exception and soon let him go.

And indeed, after the father repeated twice or thrice that he loved the girl and held her awkwardly close to his legs—as her frightened eyes stared out of a pale, tear-stained face encircled by the hairy fatherly arm—his ID was handed back to him and the two were allowed to go back home.

The women waited a while longer, but the father did not come out again; he must have given up his intention to go somewhere. And it was better so: when Jewish people celebrated Passover in Hebron, it was definitely not a day for Arab people to be going about their business there.

## *A Boy*

As soon as the spanked-girl incident had concluded peacefully, the three women became aware of a commotion from another incident, very close by. They moved there. It took place at a checkpoint called the Pharmacy Checkpoint—named after a pharmacy that used to occupy the ground floor of an apartment building there; a bleak sign over its barred front still attested to its past existence and present demise.

This new incident, too, involved a child. He was older than the girl, perhaps old enough to be called a youth. A youth, then. This youth sat next to the checkpoint sentry box, his hands restrained behind his back in plastic cuffs, his eyes bound in a strip of cloth. About a dozen soldiers in helmets and thick bulletproof vests encircled him, some of their weapons pointed in his direction and others at the few passersby who gathered around. A few minutes later some of the soldiers took up position with their rifles pointed toward a yelling woman—who must have wanted to free the youth or at least approach him—and they stood there as a tight wall between her and him.

In the meantime several jeeps had arrived on the scene, probably alerted by one of the many radio-communication devices with antennas sticking out of the soldiers' uniforms and rucksacks. The youth remained inside the ring of soldiers. His blindfolded expressionless face and his whole being seemed fragile, frail, compared to his captors. They were bigger not just because of their age but mostly because of all the gear that made their torsos look broader, bulkier, and longer, though when they inhabit their other, civilian world—private and intimate—these captors' torsos may actually be quite slender, like that of their captive.

The three women—visibly upset, and one of them, not the woman recording this story, even burst into tears—approached the three Israeli police officers who were still on guard nearby, although two had seated themselves for a break on the hood of their police van. The women asked them whether they didn't think they were obliged to intervene in this incident as well and protect the rights of the minor sitting there shackled, blindfolded and threatened by weapons. They answered that no, they didn't, for the army was present and it was sovereign here, and they were its subordinates, not the other way around.

When the three women returned to the checkpoint, they saw that the youth had been raised to his feet and was now being dragged and pushed into one of the jeeps, to the sound of the yelling woman who was still trying to approach him so as to pull him loose. She was joined by the people crowding round, whose number and agitation were growing. The incident seemed about to develop into a veritable security clash, but the soldiers hung on and gave the jeep driver a moment to start the engine and rev it up. Soon it screeched off with the soldiers and their young captive sitting inside.

An infinitely courteous army officer at the scene promised the three women, who once more found themselves intervening in vain, that the youth—the boy, he said—would return right away: he would only be taken on a short ride to scare him a bit since he had been caught throwing stones—for despite being young and slight he still could have killed someone—and he would not be turned over to the police but would be brought back safely in half an hour.

An hour passed, then two, and the youth—Ahmad Younes al-Atrash was his name, and he was about fourteen at the time, as the three women learned from his father, who had been summoned and arrived in the meantime—did not return. Phone inquiries informed the women that he had been taken for interrogation to the nearby Kiryat Arba settlement police station. The three women drove to the Kiryat Arba police station, stood for a while in front of its locked gates, and drove back to their homes.

Ahmad Younes al-Atrash spent that night at the Kiryat Arba police station. The next day he was taken to Ofer prison, and his father was summoned to pick him up and take him. He went and got his son back in return for 1,000 shekels, a guarantee that the youth would show up for trial if summoned.

During the time that the three women persevered, doggedly attempting to keep track of the boy's situation, he was not summoned to trial, nor did the father get back his 1,000 shekels.

Eventually both their desire to know and their perseverance flagged.

# The Gaza Strip

# Lamenting Her Unseeing Eyes, Winter 2011

She had never faced this kind of blocked crossing. But she didn't mean to cross it anyway. She only went there to pick up—and later bring back—a nearly blind young woman from the town of Jabalya in the northern Gaza Strip, who needed medical treatment at a Ramallah hospital.

It was a Thursday in February 2011 when she drove out to get the young woman and her mother. The drive from Jerusalem to the crossing lasted under an hour and a half. South of Ashqelon Junction, road signs had become infrequent, although there were still several recreation and touring alternatives to proceeding to pick up an unknown patient.

At Yad Mordechai Junction, for example, the woman at the wheel could have turned left and enjoyed fresh coffee and pastries at the service station coffee shop. Or she could have turned right to Kibbutz Yad Mordechai to honor the memory of Mordechai Anilewicz, commander of the Warsaw Ghetto Uprising. To stand at the foot of his colossal memorial sculpture rising against the background of the iconic water tower shelled in 1948, and then visit the site that reconstructs the Egyptian army attack. Visitors are invited—this she heard from an Israeli mother who had accompanied her daughter on a school trip there—to climb onto tanks and enter trenches like the local fighters back in those days. After that she could pay a visit to the Yad Mordechai Museum, "From Holocaust to Revival," and try to rediscover that connection. (As a child she heartily embraced it, but later the connection loosened and eventually was severed altogether.) She could finish up with a visit to the Bee and Honey House, observe a real beehive, and taste honey without thinking of the sting.

But the woman at the wheel turned neither left nor right but proceeded across the plain in her car, south past the sign indicating the entrance to Netiv Ha-Asara, and on—straight on, straight on. It's a good asphalt road, a smooth black strip between shiny yellow margin lines, one side lined with trees, the other a lush meadow, and she on her own in a red Ford Fiesta, the only car on the road. A pale blue sky stretched over it all with white feathery clouds on the horizon, clouds that in a short while would become the background for the end of the journey. It was coming up, the end of the journey. Her eyes already saw a cluster of tall electricity poles and structures, not yet identifiable.

"Erez Crossing" was written in Hebrew, Arabic, and English on a road sign. It was a large sign, and only its upper third was filled with the writing and arrow pointing to the left. The other two thirds were left blank, meaning, beyond this lies nothing. A closer look at the dark green sign, however, revealed remnants of white Arabic lettering: there must have been more writing here in the past, and it was erased, along with the possibilities it may have offered to drivers and passengers.

But this woman at the wheel had no other destination

anyway, only Erez Checkpoint. She followed the sign to the left, then, and feared the unknown. Having turned, she was greeted by another sign on her right, white-painted metal affixed to three posts. "Welcome to Erez Crossing," the clean sign said cordially with its handsome blue lettering in all three languages—Hebrew, Arabic, and English. She stopped next to it and looked beyond it through her window, at a medium-height barbed-wire fence not far off, its lower part vertical and its upper part at an angle, and at the gray concrete wall behind that, much taller, and at another barbed-wire fence that crowned it, making it look even taller, it too with its lower part vertical and upper part at an angle, in perfect harmony with its lower counterpart. Then she looked over the galvanized tin roof of an elongated rectangular structure standing behind all these fences, most of it hidden by the wall and only the dark rectangles of its windows lined up looking out of a whitewashed wall. Then she continued driving.

Just a bit farther. For the road was blocked by concrete barriers that only allowed her to turn right toward a spacious parking lot, there at her convenience free of charge. She got out of the car, and with the quiet, generous vastness all around she stretched pleasurably and relaxed her body, made stiff by driving. The gentle air of a southern sunny winter day caressed her face and filled her lungs. Another relaxed moment or two went by, until she remembered where she was and why she had come here, and the stolen pleasure of relaxation was gone.

Since the last time she was here, nearly two decades ago, the place had changed entirely. She was very surprised by the silence and order and clean geometry of straight lines, squares, and rectangles which replaced the bustle and disorder that used to reign here. The confusion of people and things, the improvised food and soft-drink stands and all the goods and wares, useful as well as useless, and the army jeeps and the dusty pickup trucks and jalopies and fancy limousines, and the horses and donkeys hitched to carts, and the armed soldiers checking IDs and documents of passersby face to face.

Now in the marked parking spaces of the lot stood about two dozen cabs and private vehicles, their engines silent and their drivers silently smoking beside them or talking quietly with one another. Under a tin roof sat a few elderly people on benches, bags and suitcases at their feet. Their eyes followed the woman who passed by them. None of them addressed her.

She headed toward the crossing itself. Beyond the concrete barrier the asphalt surface split into exit and entry lanes closed with electric gate-bars and covered by a large open metal structure with a blue roof; modest white pavilion stood on the right side. Inside the pavilion a young secretary sat alone in front of a computer, and a glass pane separated her from those wishing to cross into the Gaza Strip. But no one wished to enter the Gaza Strip just then. Farther on was a fenced asphalt area and a yellow sign warning of cross traffic, and there was also a marked pedestrian crossing to protect pedestrians from vehicles. But the asphalt surface itself was empty too, and the elongated rectangular structure behind it looked sealed and impermeable. The woman had nowhere else to go, so she stood next to the pavilion, alternately looking at the secretary and the structure, and waited.


She waited for the nearly blind young woman and her mother. She did not know them, but she knew their names. We shall call them Reem and Iman. She also knew a few details about Reem and why she was here to pick her up: Reem was then twenty-four years old and diabetic. She was suffering from glaucoma and urgently needed surgery to try to save what remained of her vision. She had an appointment for that day at the Ramallah ophthalmology hospital. It was her second appointment, because she had not shown up for her first one, a month earlier.

She had not shown up because there were several crucial arrangements to be made with various authorities and not all of them worked out. The family had to submit an application along with medical documents to an authority called the Palestinian Civil Committee. This committee—consisting of a single Palestinian bearing the title Health Coordinator—was authorized by the State of Israel to coordinate the exit of Palestinian patients from the Gaza Strip into its territory. The family submitted the application with the necessary medical documents. The committee was supposed to pass the application and the medical documents on to the Israeli authority, called District Coordinating Office, authorized to issue exit and entry permits to the besieged residents of the Gaza Strip. The one-man committee submitted the application with the medical documents to the Israeli authority. But the latter kept silent and gave no response. And in the meantime, the date of the operation came and went.

The Ramallah hospital rescheduled.

Once again the family submitted an application with the necessary medical documents to the one-man committee, and once again the committee submitted them to the DCO. And the DCO kept silent again. So the family applied to the Israeli organization called Physicians for Human Rights, which helps patients who have been denied certain rights, and this association applied to a more specialized authority called the Humanitarian Hotline located at the DCO. But in spite of its promising title, no response came from this authority, either affirmative or negative. The new date was about to be missed again, and Reem's eyesight was deteriorating.

At this point the woman who had come to pick up Reem and her mother at Erez Crossing—herself a long-standing eye patient whose sight had been saved for the time being by sophisticated modern medicine—decided to try her luck. She appealed to a certain member of the Knesset who, like his party, put human rights at the top of his agenda. The MK cooperated readily. He promised her that just as his office had pulled strings for ill patients and other unfortunate Palestinians, it would do so in Reem's case. Regrettably, however, even his efforts were vain. The days flew by and no answer came. Only two days remained until the appointed date.

The woman decided to try her luck once more and turned to a journalist. And there, wonder of wonders, fortune smiled. The journalist demanded an explanation from the authorities, and the authorities promised him their answer within a single day—and kept their promise: the next morning, one day before the scheduled operation, they informed the journalist that Reem and her mother were to receive their permit to exit the sealed gates of the Gaza Strip and enter the sealed boundaries of Israel, and exit these again on their way to Ramallah, in the West Bank.

The journalist delivered these happy tidings to the woman, she shared them with the Physicians for Human Rights, and this organization informed the family. But the matter was not yet settled. Apparently none of the above people were authorized to inform the family of anything. The law, perhaps for the purpose of military security, stipulates that patients approved to exit the Gaza Strip for medical treatment do not receive their final document before 7:00 p.m. on the eve of their journey. And indeed, at 8:00 p.m. Reem's father had told the woman that permission had been granted and the next morning she could pick up his wife and daughter on the Israeli side of Erez Crossing.

This is what had happened before that wintry Thursday morning when she stood confused, tense, and alert at the Erez Crossing compound in its present form, an obtrusive would-be border crossing between two states, next to the pavilion with the single secretary inside, and stared at the elongated rectangular structure beyond the platform, from which the two women were expected to emerge. For many moments no one appeared. Then they began to come out, the people from Gaza. One by one, two by two, most of them quite old, some parents with little children, and here and there, noticeable for their different appearance, gentlemen in suits who looked like businessmen.

The woman watched this sparse procession slowly making its way across the asphalt to the fence and the narrow exit turnstile fixed in that fence, not far from the pavilion where she stood. Suddenly she was gripped by an immense weight of distress. She was only now actually awakening to the reality of this place, a reality that is absurd, mad, a nightmare. The people beyond the fence seemed to be emerging from a void, a black hole. As if there weren't, and couldn't be, one and a half million human beings behind that sterile elongated rectangular structure that protruded in the middle of nowhere instead of the bustling checkpoint that used to be here.

At the checkpoint that used to be here, life had been cha-
otic, distorted, warped, but still it was life. Now, though, she
felt that in the many years she could no longer enter the Gaza
Strip, which she used to do quite often, that densely populated
strip of earth had become a kind of phantom kingdom, and its
inhabitants who dropped out of sight had also dropped out of
mind and lost their human faces.

Israel's "disengagement" from Gaza had happened, and particularly the detachment and mortar shells and Qassam rockets
and missiles and assassinations and "Summer Rains" and "Cast
Lead" (both appellations of Israeli military offensives), and
photographs of bombings and rubble and anonymous figures
wandering or rummaging around in it. And statistics came,
terms and concepts: 61 percent suffered from food insecurity.
Another 40 percent were now unemployed. Between 95 and
100 percent of the water from Gaza's aquifer was now undrink-
able. The "blue baby" syndrome. Anemia.

In the past, inside the Gaza Strip, amidst the unemploy-
ment and poverty and water shortage, the woman had known
people with faces and life stories, young and old, men and
women and children. She had strolled with them on the beach,
dashed around with them in town and along refugee camp
alleys, found shelter in their homes, and even in homes of total
strangers who, tugging her arm, saved her from flying stones
and the black smoke of burning tires and the white fumes of
tear gas, and rubber ammunition and live bullets. She had
drunk and eaten with them and heard their stories, sad stories
but nonetheless juicy and often seasoned with humor. She had
discovered a whole world there, a strange and distant world
that became less frightening with time, actually became familiar and close, familiar and comprehensible despite controversy,

close despite differences, a world—even when hostile—neither locked nor blocked.

In the Gaza Strip the woman had learned to cross borders. Not ideological borders but human ones, both real and imagined. She learned to loosen and break down barriers, outer and inner ones, to subject anxieties and prejudices to mockery. She learned to surrender to curiosity rather than to fear. And thus she had tasted precious personal freedom, more special than all other kinds of freedom, found even in harsh times of conflict and war, of brainwashing and of shrinking back, hedgehoglike, to which she herself, in spite of her humanist worldview, was not immune—not at all.

Then fences were erected around the Gaza Strip, gaps sealed, and she no longer returned to Erez Crossing and to the Palestinian people behind it. Even her phone conversations with them gradually ceased, the voices grew silent, images blurred, scents faded. The checkpoint won.

And the people disappeared from her view. She knew that Haidar Al-Shafi had died in the meantime, that R. escaped to Egypt with his wife and children, that H. somehow made it to Syria and then Lebanon, and S. reached the USA, and the rest probably remained imprisoned between the fences and the sea.

And now the second millennium was over, and with it the sixty-one years of her life partner's life; and the third millennium had begun, and its first year saw the end of the sixty-five years of her only sister's life; and its sixth year brought the end of the ninety-six years of her mother's life, during which Israel's wars were added to the two world wars she had experienced, those wars of Israel that never ceased despite all the peace-seeking efforts her mother had participated in; and in the tenth year of this millennium she herself, daughter of that strong, stubborn, and determined mother who had died brokenhearted, was now in the middle of her seventh decade of life, and now she was here again, at Erez Crossing, which—just a few years before all these disasters befell her—had been a milestone in the course of her life.

And now she sees people from Gaza again. Under very different circumstances.

They were few that sunny winter day. Few and silent, their movements cautious, their clothes clean and tidy, even somewhat festive, and their things packed in bags and suitcases. From afar one could almost imagine them as tourists on vacation. Even close up they did not show signs of food insecurity or the saltiness of polluted aquifer water; at most one could perceive some patients' health problems—one limped, another was rolled along in a wheelchair, another leaned on someone who accompanied her.

The woman hung on to her memories and wished to approach these people, hold out her hand, greet them with a smile. But there was no call for such gestures here. The people exiting the elongated rectangular structure crossed the yard and crowded with their luggage between the turnstile bars of the last fence, turned each in their own direction to the waiting cars and taxicabs.

At long last Reem and Iman exited too. The woman recognized them by Reem's blindness. The young woman wore dark glasses and the older one held her arm, her other hand carrying a heavy, bulky black bag. They crossed the yard and approached the turnstile. The mother helped her daughter get in between the turning metal bars, entered behind her, and got stuck because of her bag—it was too bulky for the narrow turnstile. Someone came from behind and helped extricate it by pulling hard. The mother and daughter got through, and the helper opened a regular gate in the fence through which he passed with the bag, then handed it to them.

Now the woman could hold out her hand and smile. But the two were in no mood for greetings and smiles. The daughter's face was blank, the mother's tired and tense, and they shook the waiting woman's hand listlessly and walked with her to the car. The mother placed the bag in the trunk, helped the daughter into the backseat, and settled herself beside the woman at the wheel, and they immediately got on their way.

The woman at the wheel offered them some chocolate she had brought along, and then realized she had forgotten the younger woman was diabetic. Then she suggested they have a cup of coffee at the service station, and realized that the mother was afraid to be late—they had already lost so much time at the checkpoint. The woman at the wheel offered to play some music, a Fairuz or Umm Kulthum CD, got no reaction—had no idea whether they wanted it or not. The rear-view mirror reflected a face smiling shyly, politely, from the backseat, and a self-conscious smile on the worried face of the mother in the front passenger seat revealed her missing teeth.

The tones of the opening orchestral bars of Umm Kulthum's *Inta 'Omri*, slow and restrained at first and then growing stronger, sweeping and intoxicating, only kept the woman at the wheel from hearing what the mother seemed to want to tell her. She turned the player off. She thought: *What's to be done?* She was driving two depressed women from the Gaza Strip, she couldn't simply give them pleasure and share it with them as she did with the women from West Bank villages whom she occasionally smuggled to the beach. She thought: *It's all so obvious*, what was there to hear that she couldn't figure out herself?

Still she made an effort to understand Iman's Gazan dialect. Iman told her about Reem's blindness that had recently put an end to her university studies. She spoke about the decision to undergo surgery, about the missed first appointment, about the long wait for an exit permit for a new date. She spoke of the long wait at the crossing, the humiliation of Reem's repeated body searches, when something kept beeping, probably a belt buckle. Then she spoke a little about the family's life in the Gaza Strip. About the impacts of war that had forced them to vacate their damaged home, about the father, now unemployed, who had worked in Israel for years, about hours and days without electricity and water, about buying expensive bottled water, about the faulty medical treatment of her daughter's illness, about the shortage of medication, and about the other children who were growing up and studying but had no chance of finding work. She lamented.

It was a helpless lament full of despair, a mere hour and a half from Jerusalem.


They passed Jerusalem and reached the enormous Qalandiya Checkpoint north of the city, where they had to cross over into "Judea and Samaria" on their way to Ramallah. Before actually reaching Qalandiya Checkpoint they encountered nasty traffic jams and pedestrians hurriedly winding their way among cars and fences. One almost suffocates here, yet one feels no desire to stretch one's limbs and take a deep breath. The woman at the wheel left her car in an improvised parking lot in front of the checkpoint, for she could not cross the checkpoint with them on board. They trudged on foot toward the checkpoint. Reem held on to her mother's arm, and the driver and the mother carried the large bag between them. The woman crossed the checkpoint with them. Theoretically it too is closed to her by force of some military regulation, but in fact, unlike Erez Crossing, this crossing has loopholes. And they are used: people crossing north into "Judea and Samaria" are often ignored, while only those crossing south into Jerusalem, and especially the Palestinians among them, are inspected. She could thus accompany Reem and Iman in a cab from Qalandiya to the Ramallah hospital, leave them there to their fate, and get home safe and sound. In order to remain human in this place one needs to violate several regulations and be aware of others.

Reem underwent three or four surgical procedures, and they failed. The doctors at Ramallah could do no more to save her remaining eyesight, and three weeks later the woman was asked to drive the two women from Qalandiya Checkpoint back to Erez Checkpoint.

Once again she stood and watched the exit gate at a checkpoint insolently pretending to be a border crossing between two states, and again she waited, heavy-hearted. This time she dreaded seeing the look on Reem's young face—it would now be even more blank and grim than before. Significant time passed after Iman informed her by cell phone that they had entered the checkpoint compound, but the two were not yet visible among the emerging multitude. Calls to their phone were not answered either. Finally the woman lost her patience and did what she had not been able to do at the Erez Checkpoint: she entered the compound.

Inside, the vast pavement was crisscrossed with tall barbed-wire fences, some of them demarcating narrow passages, "sleeves" in checkpoint jargon. She threaded her way into one of these and looked for the mother and daughter among the people crowding inside, waiting for their turn to enter the electrically-controlled turnstiles one by one. In vain. The two were nowhere to be seen. A soldier behind one of the glass panes remembered the blind young woman and her mother. He told the woman that he did not let them through because their entry permit into Israel was no longer valid. He had no idea where they were now; perhaps they went to the DCO at sleeve no. 5 in order to arrange for a new permit.

She went to the DCO in sleeve no. 5, but it was closed.

Again she elbowed her way into the waiting lines and moved along with them from sleeve to sleeve—from one sleeve that would suddenly close to another that would suddenly open—until within one of the queues she almost literally stumbled against Iman's large bag. The mother stood there with her daughter, holding two green IDs and documents, and cried. Reem stood next to her, head bent, holding on to her arm.

This is what had transpired: The State of Israel's Ministry of the Interior issued permits to enter Israel for Reem and Iman, valid only for that Thursday three weeks ago, from 5:00 a.m. until 7:00 p.m. "Exit for purposes of hospitalization," it said. But this hospitalization lasted—as hospitalizations usually do—more than fourteen hours. The mother had not read the permits, and three weeks later when she reached the inspection window behind the electrical turnstile with her daughter, the soldier behind the secured glass pane tore up the two official forms that were now null and void, and instructed the two women to turn back. Iman refused: she wanted to go back home with her daughter, to the town of Jabalya in the Gaza Strip. They had nowhere to turn back to, no one in Ramallah. As she persistently refused, the soldier yelled at her to get lost, she and her daughter. He didn't explain anything. He wasn't even able to speak to her in her own language. Finally someone from the waiting line had volunteered to take them to the DCO, and there they were immediately issued new permits for that day, from 5:00 a.m. to 7:00 p.m. When the woman met them, the mother was holding the new permits, and they were allowed to cross the checkpoint.

All this Iman told her later in the car, on a drive that took a long time along roads heavy with Thursday-afternoon traffic. She spoke and wept. She needed time to calm down from her frightful checkpoint experience, and the notion that she and her daughter might have to remain overnight without shelter, as well as her humiliation by that young soldier, younger even than her daughter. She also wept over her dashed hopes, wept for Reem's blind eyes, for which no cure was found. And she calmed down only after her phone rang again and again and family members asked how the two of them were and where they were exactly at that moment between Ramallah and Gaza. It was obvious that Iman was glad to be going home. She took out a pack of candy from her handbag and offered some to the woman at the wheel. And smiled at her: they did have a home in the besieged Strip, and people who cared about them were expecting them.

When they arrived at Erez Crossing it was already nearly 7:00 p.m. There was no one in the transit pavilion. A few people waited, pacing to and fro; two little children ran around on the road, empty of cars, and a young couple was even strolling arm in arm. A full moon winked at them from the night sky. As soon as the head of a secretary appeared in the window, a short but crowded waiting line formed. Iman hurriedly freed her daughter's arm and ran to stand in line so they wouldn't miss their 7:00 p.m. exit deadline, God forbid.

Reem bent her head and continued standing in place, helpless. The woman stood next to her, stroking her shoulders. The young woman lifted her blind face to her in a sad smile. Iman came back holding the signed papers, hugged the woman tightly, kissed her on both cheeks, and invited her to visit them at home in Jabalya. She gripped Reem's arm, lifted the black travel bag, loaded it on a small luggage cart (available to her this time), and turned toward the fence. Israeli workers there, digging a ditch under brilliant work lights, helped her get around the ditch with her daughter and pushed the cart toward the gate for her, and it immediately opened to receive the women returning home to the ghetto. To a family with thirteen sons and daughters and thirty-two grandchildren. Iman waved to the woman one last time from the platform and then was swallowed up along with Reem into the long rectangular structure. The woman imagined that she could hear Iman sighing with relief.

A while after the woman returned from this trip to Erez Checkpoint she sat down on the floor of her study and pulled out the many cardboard boxes on the bottom shelf of her cabinet, filled to bursting with newspaper clippings she had collected over the years and articles she had written, most of them before the onset of the computer age. She looked through them and found the file with notes and clippings and letters from the years when she had often visited the Gaza Strip. She took them out and leafed through them; most had been typed on an electrical typewriter and some of them printed on a dot-matrix printer's "tractor paper rolls." She sifted through these and the newspaper clippings and handwritten letters, only glanced at them, didn't really read them. Her heart refused to read.

But she did not return them all to the shabby binder either—it could no longer be closed anyway. She placed them in a pile on the floor at the foot of the cabinet. Now when she washed the floor she had to pick up the pile, gather the pages and notes and bits of newspaper that dropped from it, reassemble them in a loose bundle, and place the bundle on her desk. But even there it was a nuisance. Finally one day she packed them all in a new brown cardboard file, wrote on the cover in black ink what had been written on the cover of its predecessor, "Gaza. Materials to be sorted," and placed the file on the narrow blue couch in her study.

More time went by and she sorted it out, and then read it all too. She read once, twice, and reminisced and was agitated and filled with pain and fury—and longing. Yes, she longed for those days when her world was more intact. And apparently so was the world of the protagonists of her stories and of the writer of the letters. And she didn't stop until she had retyped some of these stories and saved them in computer folders and files, and somewhere in the cloud.


These stories are included here as they were written, in the first person. They were written during the First Intifada. She has added a prologue and several clarifications, and memories and various facts she has discovered in the meantime. And how the story of the Gaza Strip is not over and done with but has rather gone from bad to worse. And also just a tiny bit of all she thinks about this.

# GAZA STRIP IN THE
# FIRST PERSON

# Prologue, 2016

Gaza Strip: an ugly, dense collage of dire poverty, despair, violence, cruelty, killing—this is the one and only image of the Gaza Strip in the minds of the majority of the Israeli public. The emotional reaction to it too is a single one: fear, revulsion, hatred. That's how things are, that's how they always were.

On the eve of the first uprising in the Occupied Territories, in December 1987, publicist and journalist Gideon Samet wrote an article on Gaza in the *Haaretz* daily newspaper following a series of assaults against Israelis in the Gaza Strip. The writer harshly criticized the Jewish settlers there, who "entangled us with their pointless settlements in the heart of one of the world's most densely populated Arab areas." But the essence of his rage was directed at that very same "Arab population": "The hell with Gaza. . . . Let the Gazans boil in their own juices," he wrote viciously, toxically. "That great find, Gaza, should be handed over to the Egyptians, let them choke on it. . . . Who needs that black hole . . ."

Black hole, *sic*. Thousands of human beings living right next to Israel and subjected to its rule are rendered null and void by a stroke of the pen. Worse still: a hole. Worse still: a black hole.

From 1987 until 1991 I often visited the Gaza Strip. It was

never a black hole. Israel was doing its best then, as it had earlier, to turn it into just that. And never succeeded.

It didn't succeed later either—not by closure nor by siege, nor by shelling it from the sea, the air, the ground. People live there. Live—that is, they're born, grow up, find partners, have children, grow old. Lives filled with destruction and suffering, but still with some hours of joy. As most human beings live, who, great as their trouble may be, persist in maintaining a routine of some sort. And no life routine is devoid of pleasant moments, even joyous ones, even happy ones.

> For even there, next to the chimneys, in the intervals between the torments, there was something that resembled happiness. Everyone asks only about the hardships and the "atrocities," whereas for me perhaps it is that experience which will remain the most memorable. Yes, the next time I am asked, I ought to speak about that, the happiness of the concentration camps.
>
> Imre Kertész, *Fateless*, https://www
> .goodreads.com/work/quotes/309125
>
> Translated by Tim Wilkinson, published
> by Vintage International, 2004

That is what the Jewish Hungarian writer Imre Kertesz wrote at the end of his autobiographical work *Fateless*, about the year he spent in Auschwitz.

No, the Gaza Strip is no death camp. That is an impossible and superfluous statement. But for very many years, and increasingly, it has been a huge concentration camp—this is very much a possible and obvious statement. A strip of land choked, enclosed, and besieged from all sides and devastated by wars. A place perpetually inhabited by destruction and death. Therefore the profound, surprising, amazing human truth of Kertesz's words applies here as well, just as it has in many other places in the world where suffering has been the constant lot of most of the population.

Nearly two million human beings live in the Gaza Strip today. Two million people who will never be null and void, never a black hole. One merely needs a point of view that sees people. One that does not see them is warped, at first uncurious, then blank and eventually blinded, either by ideology or by fear and weakness.


We were two women drawn to the Gaza Strip ever since our very first visit there in the autumn of 1987, two women from Jerusalem: Edit Doron, a linguistics scholar, and myself. Every few weeks we would travel by car together from Jerusalem. We would drive about an hour and a half to Erez Checkpoint, park the car on its Israeli side, and on the other side meet the Gazans whom we had arranged to visit.

Several months after we began our visits there, after we had greatly expanded our circle of friends and acquaintances in Gaza, the First Intifada broke out. The start of this popular uprising was signaled at Jabalya refugee camp in the northern Gaza Strip on December 8, 1987, after an Israeli truck driver accidentally hit two taxicabs transporting workers from the camp. Four of the men were killed. This incident ignited a mass revolt that had been fermenting for years, under the harsh conditions in the Strip—personal, social, and economic.

The unbearable living conditions of Gaza Strip residents in the 1980s were described in detail in the book *Intifada* (Schocken, 1990) by Ze'ev Schiff and Ehud Ya'ari. Among other causes, the writers stated that some months before the uprising broke out, a secret report about the dire state of affairs in the Gaza Strip had been placed on the desk of the coordinator of the Government Actions in the Territories. Its title was "The Gaza Strip until 2000." Schiff and Ya'ari cite this document among others to show that the Israeli leadership should have expected the uprising and not been surprised by it—as it actually was.

The report, 218 pages long, was written by professionals: an urban planner, an economist, and a sociologist. It is a dry factual study, comprising mostly data, numbers, and tables. To stress their point, Schiff and Ya'ari formulate the conclusion drawn from this research in a quite different tone, direct and blunt:

> Although the writers of the report, and the officers who wrote its introduction, avoided making unequivocal summaries and recommendations to the political echelons, no reader could escape the grim conclusion that before long the Gaza Strip will become a human "time bomb," a cancer spreading through the body of the State of Israel. Even if only a few of the study's prognoses materialize, clearly the moment will come when Israel will be on its knees, pleading for someone else to take the Gaza Strip away with all its trouble, help Israel rid itself of this wasps' nest.

Time bomb, cancer, wasps' nest. Not women and men and children, not mothers and fathers, brothers and sisters, grandfathers and grandmothers. Not a community and its individual members. Israelis did not see this, not even the harshest critics of Israeli policy in the Gaza Strip. Schiff and Ya'ari's description of the policy of oppression and humiliation under Israeli military rule in the Gaza Strip shows that the writers are among those harsh critics, for their descriptions are a damning indictment of the Israeli elite—both military and political. But when Schiff and Ya'ari wished to move their readers, they too resorted to images borrowed from the realms of violence, disease, insect pests.

To the uprising, whose main tools were mass demonstrations, stone throwing, tire burning, and strikes, the Israeli army responded with unbridled violence, beatings with fists and truncheons and rifle butts, harassment, incursions into homes, gunfire, and curfews. Everyday life in the Gaza Strip worsened. Streets and alleys were filled with black smoke from burning tires and white billows of tear gas. The numbers of dead and wounded mounted progressively.

These were the circumstances under which Edit and I organized a tour of the Gaza Strip for Israeli writers and artists in early January 1988. Many of the people we tried to interest in coming were afraid, some canceled at the last minute—but nineteen people did show up. They came wanting and needing to witness the situation firsthand, to find out for themselves about the suffering inflicted on the inhabitants and the extent of oppression exerted by the State of Israel and its army—and in their name as citizens of the state. They returned from this tour like people coming back from the end of the world. The impressions they later published in the press are preserved in my files—faded, tattered, forgotten, as newspaper clippings end up being.

# Abandon All Hope, Ye Who Enter Here, January 1988

"Abandon all hope, ye who enter here," wrote poet Meir Wieseltier in his article, inspired by the inscription above the gates of Hell in Dante Alighieri's *Inferno*. All the participants of the tour were shaken and shocked by what they saw and heard where their Gazan hosts drove them, places that all of them were visiting for the first time in their life. Most of them probably for the last time, too. Shaken and shocked, but alienated. Feelings of guilt about Israel's conduct in the Gaza Strip past and present—and perhaps even more the tension and fear that distressed them throughout the tour and wrought havoc in their vulnerable minds—did not leave much room for simple human empathy.

This, at any rate, is the impression left by their writings. In spite of their good intentions, the writers—all of them articulate and powerfully expressive masters of language—seem not to have seen normal human beings but creatures of a different species. Minutiae of the inhabitants' rebellious gestures and their everyday lives, even articles of clothing, seemed to the writers strange, even grotesque sights or nightmarish apparitions.

Here:

> As from the bowels of the earth [out of nearby hovels] a mass of hell-dwellers suddenly bolts and closes in on the car. Most of them are women and boys. One of them still grips stones in both hands. And he will not let go of them. This is his infernal spasm. (Meir Wieseltier)

And also:

> Jabalya refugee camp is a mass of laundry lines stretched all over its length, breadth and diagonals, at times as wide as the dwelling shack itself. Here one sees women in traditional colorful dress, not fashionable nor groomed, only their head-kerchiefs white as snow. . . . Soon the yelling women appear, as well as a man, his head wrapped in a red-and-white *keffiya* as if suffering from toothache, and wearing a checkered dressing gown. (Dalia Rabikovitch)

And also:

> This is an endless journey, through main and side streets, alleys, meandering trails, dirt tracks, sewage puddles. . . . Groups of inhabitants hang around idly, anticipating nothing at all; perhaps waiting for the smallest spark to re-ignite them. This endlessness is an inseparable part of the harsh general picture. Like fear. Sensing there is no way out. You are led, imprisoned in the faltering car, suddenly partaking

of the fear, the suffocation, the insult, this feeling of no way out, and have no idea what the next moment will bring. You gaze out at the hostile Gazan exterior through the car window, and the hostile Gazan exterior gazes back at you, very close up, from the other side: you are part of the tension and fear and this endlessness. (Yitzhak Ben-Ner)

And also:

Jabalya. The vehicle bumps over obstacles, little sandy mounds, as if this piece of nowhere has been stuck in the middle of the desert. First, white smoke is seen billowing from the camp. . . . A helicopter hovering above showers teargas canisters into the camp. . . . Then people emerge from the white smoke, especially women and boys. An instant lies between your distinction "women" and the figure of a single woman, no longer young, who sticks her head inside the car window. Another instant and this one woman who yells and yells is reduced to a mouth; a large mouth thrust at your eyes yelling and sobbing. . . . Then the car doors are opened wide and many heads peek in, tremendous commotion. Good that someone is guilty of this distress and that someone, those someones, are not *you* [emphasis in original]. Perhaps. And another thing, the way they thrust their heads in the car, peeking beyond the seats, and farther still. It occurs to you that they want to take for themselves some of that protection suggested by the car's interior. In the meantime a man, scarred, wearing a *keffiya*, makes his way through. (Ronit Matalon)

And we, Edit and I, who did not usually get around in closed cars but walked outside with the people whom we came to know and befriend, ate with them—tiny crisp-fried sardines that Gazan fishermen had caught that night—and visited their homes, hosted them in our own homes. In the Gaza Strip we found friends and interlocutors, warm, open-hearted people who, in spite of all their hardship and suffering, showed a surprising measure of humor, black humor, wild, ironic, but also mischievous, light, and merry. They listened to us, showed interest and asked questions, wished to know about the atmosphere in Israel, opinions, expectations. And we listened to them and grew familiar with everyday life in this region that at the time was under curfew every single evening, from 8:00 p.m.; full curfew was often imposed on tens of thousands of people in its towns and camps, in this region most of whose inhabitants, nearly seven hundred thousand at the time, were not permitted to go anywhere, neither to Israel nor to other countries; a region where thousands of inhabitants spent days and months and years in prison and prison camps, and many more were beaten, humiliated, harassed in a thousand and one ways, day and night, on the street and at home. In those days it seemed there was not a single family in the Gaza Strip who had not been a direct victim of army violence.

And still we were warmly welcomed.

# R.

He was incarcerated in Israeli jails for fifteen years, from 1970 until 1985. Edit's and my acquaintance with him began with a letter he wrote from one of those prisons, Ashqelon, in March 1985. The handwritten letter was in Hebrew and filled eight large pages, a photocopy of which I keep to this day. Edit and I read this letter during our first visit to Gaza, at the office of attorney Raji Surani. We read and were captivated. What irony: we were captivated by the charm of a Gazan through his Hebrew, the likes of which is not to be found among most Israelis, not even the better educated, so precise and richly expressive. We wished to make the writer's acquaintance and were informed that very day that our request had been received. Our friendship grew quite fast, too, and the man, we'll call him R., became central to our familiarity with Gaza. We often stayed with him and his friends, strolled with him in Gaza's streets, hosted him in Jerusalem and strolled with him in its streets. When he went to prison, we visited him at his Gaza jail; when a good friend of his was jailed, we visited him at Ketzi'ot Prison.

Our friendship was a personal one, sincere and open, and lasted throughout our visits to the Gaza Strip. Then the Strip was blocked at both ends and we could no longer meet. Circumstances separated us for over twenty years. Then we met again, the three of us, this time at Edit's Jerusalem apartment, and instantly felt and knew that we were still friends. We had changed: our hair had turned white, or was dyed or had thinned—each in their style and size and manner—and each of us had had to cope with our own fate over these years, whether in Gaza or in Jerusalem or elsewhere in the world.

These pages, however, do not deal with our individual fates—neither with death nor with disease nor with troubles and joys that have befallen all three of us since then and to this day. They are dedicated to the Gaza Strip and its imprint in my life in the 1980s and 1990s, when its gates were still open to me. They are dedicated to the people I knew there, to the bits of life I got to know there.

For example, R.'s time at Ashqelon Prison. I didn't know him yet at the time, but something of his experience there became familiar to me from that letter which, although not personal, showed the sensitivity and spirit of its writer. The letter was written on behalf of all the Palestinian prisoners during the hunger strike that was declared at the time, demanding improvement of their prison conditions. R. was tortured more than once during his interrogations in Israel—this I know directly from him. But in his letter he wrote not about that kind of torture but rather about the sort of suffering that becomes torture in the long run.

For example, when a prisoner cannot wash and go to the toilet in proper hygienic conditions: "We request your honor," he addresses the minister of police in that letter, "to imagine the mental state of prisoners who wake up in the morning and have to wait for a long time before they are allowed to relieve themselves, wash their hands and faces."

For example, mentally ill prisoners are incarcerated together with healthy prisoners: "Three or four mentally ill prisoners are held in prison," R. writes, "all of whom have served close to fifteen or more years of their prison term." He named them and mentioned that these prisoners do not receive any kind of treatment at Ashqelon Prison.

In Ramla Prison, meanwhile, which does have a ward for the mentally ill, the conditions are inhumane and extremely cruel. This ward consists of a mixture of the ill and the pretending-to-be-ill, and horrific instances of violence, rape, and the like are rampant. . . . We preferred that those patients remain among us so they would not be transferred to that infernal place. Even if they do keep us up at night, not letting us rest, and create innumerable disturbances. Simple logic raises the question: What is the point of keeping such patients in prison? What possible security risk could their release entail? And finally, what punishment could possibly be worse than the state they already find themselves in?

In his letter R. also complained about the "cultural closure" imposed on the prisoners:

Most books and periodicals are banned. . . . Our own writings and creative work are confiscated during the occasional searches in our cells, and for one reason only: they contain a worldview that is political, ideological and philosophical and does not appeal to the censor. . . . One cannot ban a book, a periodical or newspaper that is subject to censure in Israel and which Israel allows to be published, unless they contain something that might impact security directly and concretely. We do not think that periodicals and newspapers such as *Al-Tali'a, Al-Kateb, Al-Biadar, Al-'Awda, Al-Mithaq, Al-Fajar, Al-Sha'ab, Al-Ittihad, Zu Ha-Derech,* etc. . . . teach people how to produce explosives or instruct them how to demonstrate or escape from prison.

R. concluded his letter: "We are aware of the fact that this strike hurts our health and our families. We do, however, expect it to weigh upon the conscience of those whose hostility towards us has not warped their minds and who still see us as human beings who deserve to be treated by fair human standards. . . . We repeat what was said in our previous letter: we will gladly welcome your visit in our prison—seeing is believing."

R. was released in May 1985, in what was then called "the Jibril deal."

He was rearrested several months after the outbreak of the Intifada and was sent to prison in Gaza. On April 13, 1988, he wrote to Edit from there:

*Shalom Edit!*

*Although I was not in the habit of writing letters during my first prison term, I now feel a strong urge to write you, and through you to the rest of the people I happened to meet and got to know, meetings and acquaintances that undoubtedly contributed to my strong and deep awareness and conviction that an end must be put to the tragic situation in which we all find ourselves, and to fulfill our common dream.*

*I follow with concern mixed with pain events outside prison, and hope that all those concerned will conclude, as quickly as possible, that sitting face to face and solving the problems of our region peacefully is imperative, to spare suffering, pain and casualties. I have no doubt that love will eventually prevail over hatred and peace will triumph over war, in spite of all this current madness.*

*I have to stop here for even the number of my written lines is restricted.*

*As for my personal state, I never imagined I would find myself in prison again. This, of course, is not exactly a pleasant experience! Still I try to make the most of my "renewed" time in jail and spend most of it reading. I wish to improve my English and have also begun learning French.*

*I hope this letter reaches you, and that you will answer me on the other side of the page.*

*Please give my warm regards to everyone. I do not forget you and hope to see you soon.*

*In friendship, R.*

About two months after this letter arrived we managed to visit R. in his Gaza prison.

# Visiting R. in Prison in Gaza, June 1988

Edit and I were permitted to visit R. in prison, with his sister. We came from Jerusalem, and she came from her home in Khan Yunes. We met her at the office of attorney Raji Surani in order to drive from there to the prison together, all three of us.

R's sister, a woman in her thirties, was dressed traditionally, her clothes modest and concealing. But her hair was uncovered, and her eyes, looking straight at us, were alert and curious. She was glad to make conversation, although interrupted from time to time by a weak cough. She said she had six children and was raising them on her own now. Her husband was in prison. He was sentenced to twelve years inside. We did not ask about conviction—what was there to ask? Perhaps he "incited" or was a member of a "hostile organization": this was the kind of thing for which military courts meted out such punishment, moderate according to their standards. I thought that in his stead I would have wished myself courageous enough to commit them.

Well, we didn't ask and she didn't tell. What she did find important to tell us was that she was very sorry for her youngest child, a three-year-old who was born after his father was im-

prisoned and now saw him only in jail. She didn't need to tell
us that besides her husband, her brother R. was in prison again.
After all, we knew this well enough and were about to visit him
with her, but we did not yet know—we heard this from her
only then—that another brother of theirs had lost his sanity
after fifteen years in jail. Thus at attorney Raji Surani's office,
we learned more specific details about R.'s family story under
the Israeli occupation in the late 1980s.[1]

As we rose to leave Raji Surani's office, the woman wrapped
her head in a kerchief and put on her long, wide robe, covering
her entire body and blurring its outline, and told us, two Israeli
women in light summer garb: "You see, now I go back inside
my tent." And added, smiling: "Don't think I was born this way.
I used to dress like you."

No, she certainly wasn't born like that, wrapped in so many
layers. She was born and grew up in a secular family, hers and
her brother R.'s. Thus she also managed to attend high school
and even graduated with honors. And still, since she married
early and had her six children, she bears her destiny living as do
most of the women in her society: not only obeying the traditional dress code but also sitting at home, mother to numerous
children and an obedient wife. Now that her husband was in
jail, she was subjugated to her husband's father, a strict, conservative man. She was forbidden to go out without his permission
and on her own. "That's the way it is" she said, humorously and
openly. "I too have a jail of my own." And indeed, after visiting

1. Many years later I was told by R. that in summer 2014, a son of this
sister was killed in an Israeli bombing. However, that sister was no longer
alive. She had died about two years earlier from the lung disease that was
plaguing her when we met.

her brother in prison she could not accept our invitation to lunch together—even without it her absence from home was too long by her father-in-law's standards.

We traveled to the prison by cab. On the way we saw the wretched streets of Gaza City. Some months earlier, when R. was still free, we had wandered in town together. Once he entered a small ophthalmology hospital with us: "Look how dirty it is, and there's no equipment, nothing," he said, and when we went back to that small street—one where no one ever completes unfinished buildings nor repairs broken street lamps nor collects garbage piling up—he said: "Look what a dump this is, all of Gaza is one big garbage dump."

When we got out of the cab we saw a mass of people in the street, children, women, and men. Most of them were standing or sitting in the searing summer sun, and some of them crowded in the few patches of shade slowly following the sun's progress, under several sheds that were put up there. From time to time long names of men resounded, chainlike, from the other side of the street, where the Gaza prison stood.

The crowd consisted of prisoners' family members, there to exercise their right to a half-hour visit with their jailed relative once every two weeks. The names resounding in the air were those of prisoners whose turn had come to see their visitors. When someone's name was called out, his visitors were allowed to cross the road and enter. There must have been doubts. For occasionally one of those waiting would cross the street, approach hesitantly and dispirited, and ask one of the soldiers or prison guards: perhaps the name of his prisoner had already been called and he didn't hear it? Some of those who asked received an answer, others were ordered away, some indifferently, others gruffly.

When our turn came to enter we squeezed, R.'s sister, Edit, and I, into a kind of prison lobby—a balcony surrounded by wire netting in the front of the building—and joined a long line of waiting women. Even if we were not yet inside the building, we were now among those waiting inside, and stood and watched the crowd outside through the metal wire netting. Now we were enclosed and they were free. In this place, however, it was hard to say with any certainty where prison began and where it ended, and anyway, since one could not see or sense freedom here anywhere, everything seemed to be one large prison.

No, not *seemed*—it was! All of the Gaza Strip is a prison, a piece of land where hundreds of thousands of people live a life of siege and imprisonment, of nonfreedom, of constant dependence on the favors of those who rule them, favors granted or denied, whether depending on circumstances or simply at the whim of someone in uniform.

Especially the whims of the uniformed: here, for example, is the prison guard behind the bars. He deigns to listen to a woman pressing her face against the wire netting and to tell her whether her relative's name has already been called—sometimes it turns out that the man is held in another prison altogether. Another woman he totally ignores, or hisses at her: "Forbidden, scram! Get out of here!"

Suddenly our line of women began to move, and moments later we were inside another lobby of the prison. This time it was a closed room, hot and stifling, and the people inside— women and men separated—waited in two lines in front of a curtain. A woman dressed in heavy layers with a small child in her arms pressed against me in the crush. The child had fallen asleep during their long wait. For the occasion of visiting his father he was wearing a festive suit, and drops of sweat were forming on his face. At some point my turn came, and I was pushed forward against the curtain by those waiting behind me. Behind the curtain in a small compartment a guard waited. She ordered me to lift up my blouse. She pulled on my bra and took a peek inside. Then she ordered me to raise my skirt. She pulled my underpants away from my body and looked inside. Then she patted me down. Then she ordered me to take off my sandals and spread my toes apart. Then she ordered me to open my mouth.

The humiliation I had begun to feel the moment we neared this building became almost unbearable. First I had wondered who was the humiliated and who the humiliator here. But now no doubt remained in my mind: This prison guard, intimately rummaging in my body and clothes, neither delicately nor roughly, indifferent, just doing her job as a matter of routine— *she* is the humiliated one. Not contemptible, but humiliated!

After the body search, Edit and I were separated from the Palestinian visitors. They exited into a neighboring space, while we were seated on a bench near the reception desk. The staff was obviously embarrassed. Our otherness was so prominent not only because we looked different but also because our presence there turned the tables, subverted the obvious rules of the place that were based on a total separation of Israelis and Gazans. Several prison guards even told us that if we had coordinated our visit for a date that was not a general visiting day, we could have been spared this whole ordeal—too bad we hadn't. But we, in retrospect, knew that it was important for us to undergo that ordeal, experience it for once from the inside, be subjected for a while to the absolute control of our fellow citizens who usually handle "them," not us.

We didn't seek any special privileges after the body search either, but they were handed to us—generously. I, for example, was asked with concern about my bag, which I had been required to leave inside the inspection compartment. Then I saw the enormous pile next to that compartment, belongings of the Palestinian women. A prison guard extricated my own small backpack and deposited it for safekeeping with the secretary at the counter. First I was allowed to take out a pack of cigarettes.

Finally, even the meeting with R. was held under special conditions. All visitors meet their prisoners in one general hall, a partition separating them from him, whereas we were let into a private room. R.'s sister was allowed to join us, and the four of us talked there in relative privacy and freedom, albeit monitored by a guard who sat quietly most of the time. When he intervened, he did so in a friendly manner, and he urged R. to tell us that prison conditions here were not so bad. R. agreed. At Ashqelon Prison things were much worse, he said.

# How We Didn't Manage to Visit R. a Second Time, August 1988

"What on earth are you looking for there?" asked the soldier at Erez Checkpoint. "You'll come back without your heads." I put one hand to my head to smooth my hair a bit—half fixing it, half to reassure myself—and told him that as far as I was concerned, under the circumstances, it was I, not he, who was responsible for my head. And we crossed the checkpoint—which only consisted of concrete cubes on both sides of the road. The soldiers were there to prevent passage in one direction only: from the Gaza Strip into Israel.

The main purpose of our trip to Gaza that day was another visit to R., who was still in prison and awaiting trial. The friends who were to come and fetch us from the Gazan side of the checkpoint were not present. Edit and I assumed that as we were late this time, they had given up on us and gone back, so we stood and waited for a cab to come by. The soldiers were no longer interested in us; they were busy with workers wishing to cross over to work inside Israel. Some workers were permitted to cross and others were not. One of those who weren't approached us, a very young fellow, nearly a boy, and showed us the small printed form, no larger than a note, he had presented to the soldiers. He had been given this form instead of his ID, which had been taken from him. He asked us what was written on this piece of paper that had led the soldiers to deny him entry.

The form was handwritten in Hebrew, something to do with taxes that we could not make out exactly. But the young man realized he was being required to pay a sum of money, a manner of levying not unfamiliar in the Gaza Strip. The exact wording of those notes and pieces of paper written in Hebrew which get thrust into the hands of Gaza Strip inhabitants, most of whom can't read them anyway, isn't particularly important. It is enough for them to know these pieces of paper control their life routine and without them they cannot get about: there is one note that turns them back to where they came from and another that lets them get on their way. But without their ID— which any soldier might seize—only a slip of paper with their name and ID number can protect them from instant arrest. This is the way things work here.

The young man was very agitated, talking in halting Hebrew, asking us to speak with the soldier, ask him to let him pass. He must get to his boss or else be fired. Speak to the soldier? What could we say to the soldier? There was nothing we could do to help, and our minds were elsewhere, but we listened to his helpless misery and expressed pity. We were embarrassed. Then we found a vacant taxicab and offered the young man a ride: he had been waiting in vain, but at least now he could make his way home free of charge. Another older worker who had been turned away joined us, and we rode together.

The older man was silent while the younger one spoke, lamenting the trouble that befell him: now he would have to wait a whole day at the military government offices, where all sorts of calculations would be made, and then they might compromise with him. But this day of work was lost.

We entered Gaza City. The cab driver couldn't find the address we wished to reach. As he drove along the streets looking, soldiers stopped the cab and asked for IDs—ours this time. They did let us continue, but the driver was already scared and asked us, politely but firmly, to get out. He understood that we were not wanted here—perhaps even less than he was.

We entered a nearby kiosk to phone our friends and consult with them. We also asked for a cold drink. When we wished to pay, the owner would not take our money. We were his guests and our expenses were on the house. We had already experienced such gestures of friendship on Gazan streets, but still both we and our hosts were constantly frightened. Fear is palpable throughout the Gaza Strip, and it increases with time, and so does tension. The friends we called came to fetch us from the kiosk, but this time they did not accompany us to the jail. They said they were afraid and let us off about a hundred meters away. We walked on our own, and arrived safely.

That was how I first came face to face with the intelligence officer at Gaza Prison, who is the main protagonist of this report. We'll call him Avram.

I had already had long phone conversations with this Avram. He was the man with whom I coordinated the previous visit. When I first called Gaza Prison to ask permission to visit R., he said I should address my request to the prisoner department of the Prison Service offices in Jerusalem. While on the phone he inquired—and I didn't know whether as provocation or out of

personal curiosity—who I was, what my connection with the
prisoner was, why I wished to visit him, what my political views
were. And all the while he abided by certain professional rules
to which he was apparently committed: "You are not obliged to
tell me anything, of course. I am asking purely out of interest.
Israelis never visit security prisoners." And I felt that in spite
of myself I was drawn into his game—I wished to visit R. in
prison and therefore needed to be nice to this intelligence officer. Nice but not overly so, keeping my boundaries.

That first time it had seemed to work. Avram was willing to
help. He had given me the name of the man I should address at
the Prison Service, and so I did. To my surprise that person told
me explicitly that Edit and I didn't need any special permission:
the prisoner was allowed to receive a visit by three people at a
time, and if his family members agreed to others coming in
their stead, we could simply do so. I was amazed: the regulations are clear cut, visiting is really easy—but if so, why that
whole exchange with Avram?

I called Avram again and told him what I had learned, to
which he responded: "First of all, only I determine who enters
the prison and who doesn't; it is not a question of getting a
permit here. Second, bring me written confirmation from the
Jerusalem Prison Service office." Choosing not to point out this
contradiction, I hung up and called the Prison Service again.
Again I was told politely that since I did not need special permission, they could not provide me with this confirmation.
I called Avram once more. He was still nice. He gave me to
understand that since he was curious to know who we were, he
would help us make this visit happen, which was of course up
to him and no one else. And still he insisted on having written
confirmation. This time the Prison Service acquiesced, wrote

out and sent the unneeded document, even sent it immediately, by telex. Avram, the intelligence officer, got busy and called me two hours later, even apologized for making me wait for two whole hours. He notified me that the visit was approved. Thus our first visit was made possible, the visit I described above. I didn't need to see Avram that time.

The second time was different. Now we were not allowed in, and so I asked to speak to him. I was told he would be called. We waited a long time. In front of the prison we saw the same sight as last time: a large crowd of family members standing on one side of the road, while on the other side stood soldiers. Having no visitor status this time, we actually didn't know where to place ourselves, and stood self-consciously in the middle, attracting the attention of both sides.

A short, scrawny soldier couldn't take his eyes off us. He had curly hair and the round face of a child. He approached us slowly, hesitating, glancing in all directions, and tried to make conversation. At first he seemed to want to tease us, make fun of us. But apparently he had an entirely different matter at heart. He wanted to bemoan the shitty situation he found himself in.

"You have no idea what kind of hell this is here," he said. "What shit. How repulsive. What am I doing here? You tell me. Does my father own a grocery here? a house? a field? Has my father ever been here at all? So what am I doing here, tell me? Why do I need this? Do you have any idea what we're told to do here? You know nothing. It's much worse than you think. It's our commanders. They're the worst. Not us. They order us to beat people up so badly they'll end up in the hospital. Break their bones. Listen to me, there will never be peace with the Arabs. The Arabs will not make peace. But I don't want to be here any longer. I can't take this anymore. My reservist friend has already been here twice, and he says he won't come back. No! Let them do whatever they want to."

These are only tiny bits of the young man's harangue. He said he was nineteen and a half, a regular soldier, from Yavne. As he spoke, another soldier approached us, even shorter and scrawnier. The first one, from Yavne, watched him with obvious unease as he came over. "Why are you here?" he said to him. "Can't you see I'm talking with these lefties?" He explained to us in a whisper that he didn't want to be overheard—he was afraid, even. Guys here hated him because he expressed unease with their practices.

But the second soldier persisted and came near. "What are you saying to them?" he demanded to know. "What lies are you telling them?"

The Yavne guy exploded: "Why, isn't it true that just yesterday we chased the *shabab* [youth] into an alley and there was a young woman standing in our way who'd done nothing, only stood there in the middle, and we beat her face in with truncheons?"

The other soldier said, "Yes, it's true."

"And isn't it true that a few days ago we beat a little boy to a pulp?"

"Yes, it's true," the other soldier said. "But that little boy threw stones at us."

The Yavne guy: "Not true, he didn't."

The other soldier: "He did." There was no disagreement about beating him to a pulp, or about his being "a little boy."

During this conversation from time to time some member or other of the Gazan families approached us to ask something. Each time the Yavne guy, not the other one, chased them off rudely, and sometimes he regretted this and called after them: What do you want? *Shu biddak?* and answered from a distance.

In the meantime I was summoned by intelligence officer Avram. He stood inside the prison compound, behind a barred window, and spoke to me in the same tone he'd used on the phone, at once reserved and familiar, courteous and sardonic, a bit nice and a bit aggressive. But the lesson he had tried to teach me on the phone was emphasized here as well: This was no question of rights and regulations—if I wish to visit, I must coordinate it with him, and this time I may have coordinated the visit with the family but I had neglected to do so with him. As for the explicit answer I got from the Prison Service, that I only needed to coordinate the visit with the family, he said, as if iterating a law of nature: "Israelis do not visit security prisoners—there is no such thing. And I do not intend to set a precedent here. You asked once, I was nice and let you do it, but if you intend to visit on a regular basis, that's another matter altogether."

I did not give in, and said that I was told by the Prison Service quite unequivocally that Israelis are no different from residents of the Occupied Territories in this respect, and if we ourselves have no criminal record we may visit prisoners charged with security offenses. Avram realized I intended to persist, and he certainly knew, too, that the Prison Service had given me correct information. So then he contradicted himself, as was his wont: regardless of the written confirmation, only he would decide whether we could visit the prison or not. He was the one on the spot. And besides, today R. had already received a family visit, so he was no longer entitled to another. Furthermore, we should know that when we came with a confirmation next time, we would not enjoy any special privileges and would see the prisoner in the general visiting area, across the partition.

When I realized I couldn't change his resolve, I asked him to pass a book on to R. He agreed and finally came out to meet me.

Now he actually faced me, sturdy and big and tall, and wished to teach me a last lesson before throwing me out: "Why are you here, can you tell me? What on earth are you looking for here? What is an Israeli like you, decent-looking and even well-educated, doing visiting security prisoners? They all want to kill you." He said this and pointed an accusing finger at an old woman who approached him hesitantly just then, wanting to ask him something.

Now I could no longer hold back. "I'll tell you why I'm here," I answered with all the anger accumulated from the sights I had seen in recent months as well as from the phone conversations in which I had forced myself to be nice—to him, this slick junior figure of authority, arrogant one moment and obsequious the next. "Yes, now I'll tell you what business I've got here. I'll tell you why I come here, and why I do many other things—I do them so that my son will never have to be in this disgusting, humiliating place where you are now."

# Facing the Sea, with H., Summer 1988

H. is a close friend of R.'s. They did time in the same jail, were incarcerated together at Ashqelon Prison. Edit and I also became good friends with H. He lives on the outskirts of Gaza City in a whitewashed one-story house, its construction still unfinished. From time to time we'd sit with him on the pavement in front of the house, have coffee, sweeten it with wafers, and chat. Thus we sat there a few days ago, he and Edit and me and a few other friends and acquaintances of his. A gathering. As on all the other occasions, we faced two adjacent landscapes: the sea and Shati refugee camp. The one provocatively spreads its vast bright blue yonder of unattainable freedom, the other spreads its vast murky faded-yellowish expanse, a different kind of provocation.

The sea and the refugee camp. The refugee camp and the sea. The sea! Oh, what a sea, what a day!

> Laughing, the sun views
> The beauty of the world
> "The light from my rays"—so it says—
> "Is there for everyone, everyone!" (Lea Goldberg)

A light sea breeze tempered the heat of the sun, and we resembled a group of seaside vacationers, joking and laughing. Yes, laughing—with a certain freedom: the freedom with which the two of us laughed rather than cried in Gaza, the freedom to cling to our discovery made possible by the people we had befriended there, who in that beaten and tortured place still possess a surprising measure of joie de vivre, an undying vitality that is strong enough at times to kindle sparks of gaiety in the heart of darkness. I recall that during one of our strolls down Gaza streets I spontaneously said to our sardonic, sarcastic fellow wanderers that something of the Jewish humor of Eastern Europe had been passed on to their fellow Gazans. And I immediately regretted this a little, for why would anyone understand this here? But I also knew that one more strangeness in this crazy situation would not make that much of a difference.

H. had spent many years in Israeli prisons. He was a boy when first arrested and an older man when set free. Like R., his personality and views were shaped in prison. His excellent Hebrew, too, was a product of his jail time. And the man is a natural storyteller. He excels in the telling details, for example in describing life under Israeli control: There's a prison guard who when leaving a cell used to bang the door with such force that it startled all the inmates, and another guard who used to close it slowly and gingerly. There's a soldier who, wishing to get your attention, slapped you on the shoulder, while another punched his fist in the back of your neck.

"These differences are important—one should differentiate between people and know that not all Israelis are the same." Thus spoke H. And I listened and thought: *Write this down, make a note of the shades of character your Gazan friends help you discern among your own countrymen.*

So here I am, writing it down.

"Imagine you're sitting in one of the interrogation rooms of Gaza Prison," H. suggested as we sat with him facing the sea on the pavement in front of his house and had coffee and wafers. "Seated on a chair, hands tied behind your back, head stuck in a stinking sack, and the soldier in charge of you won't let you sleep."

"Sleep deprivation" is the official name for this sort of torture.

"How do they deprive you of sleep? One soldier shakes your shoulder a little to keep you awake, another soldier punches his fist in the back of your neck and adds a curse—quite a difference, isn't it?"

This was one of his experiences during his latest arrest, some time before we made his acquaintance. The sleep deprivation episode had an unpleasant sequel, he told us. After several sleepless days and nights he began to hallucinate and no longer knew where he was. Then one day he was brought before a judge and released immediately, not charged with anything.

On the day he saw the judge he was near fainting, he said. He did not go into details but described his hallucinations: the sights he saw, the people he met, the colors and smells—how real it all was, he marveled. And how nice that he was now better and could tell his stories again. And how wonderful it was to listen to him, over black coffee and cigarettes, looking out at the vast blue sea, as if all's well that ends well and nothing very serious had happened then, is happening now, or ever will.

But there were others there with us, and they told different stories.

M., H.'s brother, told us: Not long ago he was arrested and taken to Ansar 2 detention camp. In the vehicle on the way there the soldiers pushed him down to the floor, kicked his face, and wounded his mouth. It was a deep and painful gash. His lips were still swollen and cracked. After eighteen months in custody he was released without being interrogated even once. No charges were filed against him either.

An Englishwoman, a photographer, told us: On her way to join us she saw a group of youngsters kneeling in the street, facing the wall of a house, while soldiers hit them and cursed. The curses were shouted very loudly, and she had the impression that more than to abase the kneeling youngsters, the curses were meant to spur on and encourage the soldiers themselves, who knew they were carrying out a despicable job—the strong abusing the weak.

A young man from Shati refugee camp told us: Often at night inhabitants are dragged out into the street and made to clean it up after clashes have taken place there during the day, or to erase slogans from walls. There was also a new regulation issued on this matter—any owner of a structure where slogans appear on the walls is liable to be fined or imprisoned, regardless of whether he lives there.

Another man told us: He and his friends are constantly required to climb up walls and electricity poles to take down Palestinian flags. If you say it wasn't you who hung them, you're told: Shut up, fucker, you piece of garbage, you piece of shit, do what you're told. And it's dangerous—one could fall and be hurt, even electrocuted.

But the slogans kept getting written, the flags hoisted. All the walls were covered with graffiti, the land filled with flags.

∗

In late summer 1988 H. vanished. Escaped. He was "wanted" and no longer willing to spend time in prisons. That was how our meetings with him ended.

Later, however, we did meet his life partner several times. She was an American Jew who came to Israel and somehow got to visit Gaza and fell in love with H., and he reciprocated and she remained in Gaza. We'll call her Ruth. When we met her I was impressed by her fluent Arabic. I remember very clearly how once we sat together in the courtyard of H.'s family home, where she lived, and those sitting with us looked for her to invite her to join us, and called out her name. And she appeared, stood there in the yard and said: "Haini!"—here I am. *Haini, haiyo, haiha* . . . I recited the conjugation to myself. And to this day, having taken steps to enrich my own knowledge of Arabic, I seek and find occasions to declare "Haini!" and recall the Jewish American Ruth and the tone of her voice back then.

We never found out what happened to H. after he escaped. Naturally, not everything was shared with us. Later Ruth too disappeared.

And then, twenty-seven years later, I saw her again. And not only her. Two of them sat there, in the summer of 2015, in the garden of my Beit Hakerem home in Jerusalem: she and her curly-haired daughter with the beautiful eyes. A little while earlier Ruth had called me, said she was in Jerusalem and would love to meet, and she had arrived with the daughter whom she and H. had had together—now about twenty-five years old.

In late 1988, by very roundabout means, H. reached Yarmouk refugee camp in Damascus, Syria, and settled there. So she told me. She joined him and they married and had this daughter. The baby's first year of life was spent in Yarmouk. Now, with the war in Syria, the camp has become an arena of killing and destruction and is nearly empty. But back then life there was still vibrant and full. And yet too difficult for Ruth, so she returned to the US with the little girl. She tried in vain to obtain an American visa for H.; since he was a former prisoner in Israeli jails, the American authorities refused to let him into the US. The family fell apart, but contact was maintained, one of love and caring, says the young curly-haired woman with the beautiful eyes, who holds on to her father's family name and navigates between her various identities: American, Palestinian, Jewish. Or perhaps she listed them in a different order. I don't exactly remember, assimilated as I am—after all, my dead life partner was German, and in those years when I traveled to Gaza he never asked me what on earth I was looking for there.

# Three Spasms, Jerusalem, 1991

## *I*

Jerusalem, Friday noon. Near the meat and poultry counter at the supermarket. Two women stand ahead of me in line at the live fish basin. One of them, a tall slim woman, her face gentle, light, pleasant, her clothes elegantly harmonized, asks for a carp. The vendor, in a no-longer-very-clean white apron, grabs a fat, thrashing carp out of the basin and shows it to the woman. She gives a satisfied nod, and forthwith he gives the fish a powerful blow with his bludgeon and the fish is still, but for a slight spasm rippling through its gills. The woman's face twists in its own sharp spasm. She shrugs, embarrassed or repulsed, and turns to the other woman waiting behind her for her own carp. But the other woman also turns her head, and the first woman gets a glimpse of the back of her neck. Just for an instant, for she immediately turns back to the vendor and the fish that lies motionless on the board, her face bright and smooth as before. The vendor guts the fish, throwing its parts deftly into an opaque plastic bag, and the buyer leans closer and points her painted fingernail to a part of the fish that was thrown into the sink. She asks him to pack that for her too.

## II

Jerusalem, another Friday. Afternoon. I go downstairs in my building and see one of my neighbors. "Oded, Oded, where are you?" he calls out to his son. I stand next to him at the entrance to the building and look around with him: Where is Oded?

There's Oded! He arrives running, panting, a cute six-year-old: "Daddy, come see what a big puddle we have in the yard, come, quick, you come too."

"What is it, Odedi, where were you?" his father asks. "We were worried, Mommy and I. I went to look for you at the playground."

"Are you crazy, Daddy?" Oded is startled. "Me go off to the playground on my own? I never go there on my own. You want me to be stabbed, killed? There are Arabs there, kidnappers, murderers! Come see what a giant puddle we have in our yard!"

His father looks at me, a spasm jerks his face. We both shrug, embarrassed or sorry.

## III

Jerusalem, another Friday. Evening. I sit with friends in a nice apartment in the Katamon neighborhood, celebrating some private occasion with them. "I was in the Gaza Strip today": I suddenly decide to tell my story to the woman seated next to me, her face gentle, light, pleasant, the jacket she wears chosen in good taste to go with the sweater under it. "I found myself in a riot in Jabalya. Someone there had raised a Palestinian flag on the dome of a mosque, and then soldiers came, and children threw stones at them and the soldiers chased the children through the alleys, chased and fired rubber-coated bullets and live ammunition. The alleys were filled with people. I saw children scattering: most of them were small, eight-, nine-, ten-year-olds. There were some wounded and two ambulances came. A child stood next to me and said: It's either the Jews or us."

The face of the woman next to me twitches in a sharp spasm: "How they hate us," she says, shrugging, embarrassed or angry, and turns her back to me, her hair washed, fragrant, flowing, and I hear her saying something pleasant to the person sitting on her other side, and chuckling.

# Being Guests in the Gaza Strip, January 1991

## *Jabalya Refugee Camp*

The gray structure was surrounded by wire netting fences between metal poles freshly painted blue. The fresh paint brought to mind a kindergarten fence. And indeed around the fence were children, many of them. From one or two hundred meters away it was difficult to see what they were doing: perhaps standing and staring at something, perhaps getting ready to move on somewhere else. Their voices were an unclear hubbub, rising and subsiding, and from time to time growing into screams.

On the right side, opposite the gray structure, was a large concrete dome, greenish in color, another structure. The minaret next to it indicated a mosque. A slim figure appeared on the dome. It climbed swiftly over the slippery rounded surface, and the next moment a Palestinian flag was flying at the top of the dome.

Now the bustle of children below grew louder. Stones flew in the air. The cluster of children moved. They ran off. They ran toward us. Now their pursuers came into view. They came into focus: soldiers in dark green uniforms, helmets, bearing their gear on their chests and backs, armed with truncheons and submachine guns. The cluster of children dispersed as they ran. They came near and now some of their faces could be seen, but it was the size of them that was most striking: they were young, some of them even very young, eight-, nine-, ten-year-olds, some perhaps twelve or fourteen at most. Only here and there did taller figures of adolescents and young men stand out.

Edit and I watched all of this from where we stood in an alley in Jabalya refugee camp, near where the commotion took place. A moment earlier other children and adolescents had blocked it with a beat-up car, making it difficult for soldiers to enter. The alley was a rather wide dirt track lined on both sides with a motley mass of low houses, structures, patches of dwellings. It was filled with people, mostly women and children. No one went indoors to seek shelter; everyone remained outside, watching the approaching tumult. There were many mothers with babies in their arms and several older and aging persons. Even when within minutes the first shots were heard the alley did not empty; people remained standing, watching and waiting. The shots grew more frequent and the soldiers chasing the children entered the alley, running and shooting.

"It's rubber," someone diagnosed next to me, in Hebrew, "and that's live ammo." The sounds of gunfire were mixed with the screams of children running away, screams of fear and the thrill of the fight. From time to time one of those on the run turned around and hurled a stone. Now ambulance sirens were heard too. Two ambulances came, picked up whoever they picked up, and sped away. Spirits among the children and boys rose even more, and the dwellers of the entire alley stood and watched.

"Aren't you afraid?"

"No," a woman answered me. "This is how it is here, every day. We're used to it." I looked at her, she smiled at me.

"No," said a fat fellow and pulled up his sleeve to reveal a long scar on his arm, "this is from a live bullet, see?" He smiled too.

"We're not afraid," they said one after the other. They did not look like heroes, the people standing there, not even particularly alert: their faces, so close to me, showed no particularly tense expression such as one might expect in the midst of a conflict with such fateful consequences for which one musters all of one's faculties. This war had become their daily routine; they had grown accustomed to it and were quite certain they had no alternative.

That day in Jabalya refugee camp in the Gaza Strip we met no tired, defeated people. We stood a few dozen meters from the whistling shots—two Israeli women among women and children and men who looked at us curiously and smiled at us, partly embarrassed, partly friendly, young and old alike, explaining—the men in fluent Hebrew—that this is their war and they will not retreat. It is a fight for their honor, their freedom, for an independent state. Slogans? Heated rhetoric? No, they said this simply, almost calmly. Not on a podium at a popular gathering nor at a demonstration but in a filthy alley in Jabalya, surrounded by the stench of open sewage and the sounds of shouts and gunfire, each one speaking in his own way. The thin child, who looked eleven years old but announced that he was fourteen, said: "It's either the Jews or us."

The Intifada was in its fourth year. January 4, 1991, was a Friday. On that day Sigal Alon, a twenty-year-old Jew from Moshav Brosh in the Negev, was killed by an Arab bus not far from Erez Checkpoint. The driver was Mahmoud Qatanghi from Jabalya. Before we took off for the Gaza Strip that day Israeli friends and people who shared our views said: Going to Gaza again? This time you've really gone mad. It's irresponsible, it's suicide. Someone even said, resentfully, almost hostile: You might hurt our struggle for peace here—you'll be killed, and what a feast that will be for the right wing.

When gunfire came very close, unknown hands pulled us into one of the buildings and seated us at a low table with others, probably inhabitants of the house, and offered us coffee. We were a bit scared and very confused, whereas they were rather amused. Perhaps we looked awkward, even ludicrous, being so helpless in the circumstances in which we inadvertently found ourselves.

Some hours earlier we had come to Jabalya refugee camp with Gazan journalists for a visit, but in the tumult and street fights that broke out, we were separated from them and got lost in the maze of camp alleys. Thus we found ourselves alone with the inhabitants, under tear gas and gunfire, and they felt obliged to protect us. Suddenly we were guests of these people, the women in colorful dresses and the elderly men in *keffiyas*—guests entitled to the hospitality required by their tradition. By the time the gunfire outside had subsided, we were already practically members of the household.

It was a thrilling moment, one of the gifts I received from my acquaintance with the Gaza Strip.

## Gaza City

After returning safely from Jabalya, that very day, we sat in the living room of an apartment in Gaza City, speaking with several people who had made time to meet us. One of them was Dr. Haidar 'Abd Al-Shafi, a physician, veteran leftist, politician, leader, a wise and endearing person. The personal acquaintance with Dr. Al-Shafi which Edit and I were privileged to make on our visits to Gaza, enjoying his company, the frank conversations we held—this was another wonderful gift I received from the Gaza Strip, another lovely Gazan personage with whom we became familiar, another human face that lit up and smiled at us, unforgettable also for its thick white eyebrows that seemed to challenge his severe high forehead and bald head, disturbing the orderliness of the man in a snow-white shirt, a tie, and tailored suit. Dr. Al-Shafi looked as though he insisted on embodying order in defiance of all the disruptions of life around him.

Haidar 'Abd Al-Shafi was then at the end of the seventh decade of his life—an elderly man, tall and good-looking, endlessly respected, even idolized. I was especially delighted, as a devout cyclist, with a story he once told us.

And this is what happened: The Israeli authorities demanded that Gaza Strip car owners change their license plates. In order to receive a new license plate, every owner had to produce a document issued by the Israeli tax authorities confirming that all taxes had been paid. Haidar 'Abd Al-Shafi argued that tying these two matters together was illegal and therefore decided to avoid using his car and began to ride his bicycle, in spite of his age and status. The Civil Administration tried in vain to persuade him to accept the rule; Dr. Al-Shafi persisted in riding his bicycle and appealed to the Israeli Supreme Court. And, most surprisingly, the court accepted the petition and ruled that the Israeli authorities' demands were indeed illegal. Consequently the license plates of Haidar 'Abd Al-Shafi's car were changed without his having to prove that he had paid his taxes.

Unfortunately, by then this arbitrary procedure had already been imposed on the majority of Gaza Strip inhabitants—of course not everyone there had the kind of prestige 'Abd Al-Shafi enjoyed, nor his resilience or humor.

What wonderful civil disobedience, I thought, and felt almost envious: if only I could combine my love of cycling down the wonderfully scenic slopes of the Jerusalem hills, through checkpoints and villages and settlements, with a brave protest against this situation that is gradually becoming an existential disaster. But two bicycle wheels and a solitary woman on a bike seat—less powerful than even Don Quixote on his Rosinante: what are they and she against an existential disaster?

Perhaps it was the presence of Dr. Al-Shafi at the meeting held after the visit in Jabalya that led our interlocutors, most of them professionals, to dress somewhat elegantly and watch their manners. At any rate, nothing about them indicated that they had all, to the very last one, been held in Israeli jails or detention camps for weeks, months, or years, or that every single one of them had been interrogated by the Shabak, or some of them had been pressured to collaborate, by whatever means.

Gentle means: you sit at a table in a room. On the table is a cup of coffee, across from you sits an Israeli man, "Captain Daoud," "Captain Daniel," "Abu Ashraf," who offers you cigarettes and coaxes you, by describing how your lot will improve if you agree.

Tough means: Your head is wrapped in a stinking sack, you are denied sleep, beaten, locked inside a "cabinet," tied up *shabah* or "banana style." These kinds of torture, according to the standard of the 1987 Landau Commission, an Israeli commission headed by an Israeli judge, are considered means of "moderate physical pressure."

This is what they told us. Someone added: "It's like secret police anywhere in the world, not a uniquely Israeli horror." Their speech was moderate, and they made sure to differentiate and be precise, even point out nuances of darkness. They felt it was important to stress that not all Israeli officials were the same, not all of them monsters. Just men "doing their job"— some intelligently, others stupidly. Some with consideration, others roughly. True, there are sadists. But at least they are not corrupt. So they said. The Civil Administration is corrupt, not the Shabak. The issue of corruption was very important to them.

And after seeing what we saw at Jabalya, we could hardly believe our ears as we witnessed such restraint, such nuanced distinctions, in this room where no one raised their voices, no one interrupted, and those sitting with us there expressed a particular wish to hear *us*, two normal Israeli women. To listen and argue with us in good humor and answer every question we posed even if it sounded naive—to explain patiently, as if trying to understand our reluctance to believe that all these horrific things actually do take place here. After all, we came from the quiet, decent streets of West Jerusalem, where life was still quite comfortable in the fourth year of the Intifada. Yes, still comfortable and routine.

However, some weeks before our visit, in the Baq'a neighborhood, near ours, in the middle of the street, two people had been stabbed to death, as well as an officer of the Border Police who tried to stop the attacker. Subsequently, as we exclaimed to our Gazan interlocutors, psychologists were sent into our own sons' classrooms, as some of their friends had witnessed the murder with their own eyes. We told them and they listened and were willing to share with us the anxiety over our two young sons, her Yoni and my Yonatan. None of the Gazans bothered to mention that two weeks before the Baq'a attack, twenty-one Palestinians had been killed by Israeli policemen during riots near the Al Aqsa Mosque. Only one of them commented with a half-smile that there, in Gaza, children were wounded and killed nearly every day, and who would think of sending psychologists to help cope with their friends' anxieties . . .

When we took leave of our hosts at that house in Gaza, Dr. Haidar 'Abd Al-Shafi said to me: "I ask you to please tell your compatriots what we said here in our talk: that in spite of everything that happens to us here, in spite of the opinions you hear or that are heard now with the Gulf crisis in the background, we here believe in the idea of two states: a Palestinian state alongside the State of Israel. We are ready to take this road to peace. Are you?"

As we made our way through Jabalya back to Erez Checkpoint, there was more rioting, and again we saw children hurling stones as soon as the soldiers arrived, armed to the teeth, from their post in the center of the refugee camp. And again shots were fired, live bullets or metal pellets with a thin rubber coating, and again there were wounded and ambulances.

This was what the war in Gaza looked like in the fourth year of the Intifada.

# Open Letter to Abu Ashraf and Those Who Send Him to Do Their Bidding, June 1991

All the names in this letter are fictitious, except for yours, which I did not make up: "Abu Ashraf." This is what you call yourself, this is how you introduce yourself to them. They are known to you by their real birth names, by their ID numbers, their addresses. They know you by the name you have given yourself, or perhaps one of your superiors has given you: Abu Ashraf.

What is your real name, Abu Ashraf? Who are you, Abu Ashraf? Where do you live—Jerusalem, Rishon Le-Tziyon, or perhaps Kibbutz Beit Alfa? I want to know your name, your identity. Your precise job. The laws and orders and instructions you follow. And I am not allowed to know. You are one of those mysterious figures whose work is done in absolute anonymity. But this work is also done in my name, and therefore I want to know who you are. And I cannot know, I cannot find out anything from you, that's just the way it is. This is in the nature of the things you do. That is the logic accepted by nearly everyone without giving it a thought, let alone questioning.

They are allowed to know that your name is Abu Ashraf. I learned this from them, as I learned that you are about forty years old, that you are rather short, a redhead, speak good Arabic—and that you're arrogant, callous, even brutal. You alternate working in Khan Yunes and Deir Al Balah. They know on what days you work and where your office is located in both places. They are summoned there from time to time. But you also make house calls: last time you visited them at the end of May.

They: I do know their names, as well as their address and their ID numbers. But I cannot reveal them, for they fear your vengeance. I met them at their home in a refugee camp in the Gaza Strip. A family: a father and mother and five sons. I saw only two of the sons; the other three were not to be seen.

And here is the family's story, in which you are a central figure at this point in their lives. The eldest son, we'll call him Ziad, about twenty-seven years old, is what is commonly called in today's Hebrew language *mevukash*—"wanted." Who knows what he's done? You probably know or think you know; you are the person authorized to know. Not I, of course. If you were accountable to me in any way, you might tell me he is a member of the "armed wing" ("shock committees"); perhaps he slaughtered or strangled collaborators or crippled them; or perhaps he is just another agitator, by your definition. Anyway, the man—be he a despicable murderer or a political leader—has been "wanted" since November 1990. And since then his family's life is no longer a life.

For some months now you have been calling on them at home time and again. At night. In varying time lapses. You come dressed in civilian clothes and are escorted by soldiers in uniform. You curse, and do it well. You brutalize, and do it well. You have beaten the father and the mother and the sons, and you have instructed your soldier-escorts to beat them. On nights when a group of soldiers arrives without you, they don't curse and beat; they only search, find nothing—and leave.

One day you ordered the family to leave its home at night. The next day, when they returned, they found all the doors to their rooms torn out of their hinges or smashed, and glass panes shattered. Even now the doors are torn out and broken, and the signs of destruction still there for anyone to see. I saw them with my own eyes.

One winter night, at the end of last year, you took the father with you, a fifty-six-year-old man, shackled and blindfolded (the mother showed me the exact gesture of shackling his hands), and drove him to Erez Checkpoint. There you ordered one of the soldiers to watch over him and to release him at 4:00 a.m. to walk back home, many kilometers away. Another night you took him to Khan Yunes. There you left him shackled inside an orange grove and told him he was allowed to walk back home.

Once you demanded to see the IDs of the father and mother, took them, told them in Hebrew "This is garbage," and tore them to bits. Now they have no IDs. They have only temporary documents. Called "Permit to Travel without ID," as if meant for vehicles, they are handwritten in Hebrew: "Required to apply new ID, original ID gone in district" (*sic*). The rubber stamps show that the holders of these strange documents are required to report every week or two and renew them. And at times they meet you in those offices where they have to report, and listen to you lecture them.

As for the fate of the other four sons, who are not "wanted": one of them, we'll call him Salah, lost his eye from a bullet in the Intifada. About three months ago he was taken into administrative detention at Ketzi'ot Prison, and he has lately been indicted for "incitement." Another son, we'll call him Walid, was taken to six months' administrative detention at Ketzi'ot Prison. Meanwhile the two sons remaining at home, we'll call them Taher and Qasem, were detained several times, sometimes interrogated about their "wanted" brother, other times not. Now they are free, for the time being. But they came out of those detentions and interrogations the worse for wear, as one used to say, in fact seriously injured by "moderate physical pressure," as present jargon has it. Eighteen-year-old Taher was arrested in mid-March this year. He was held in custody for seven weeks without being interrogated, and then underwent two weeks at the interrogation wing of Ansar detention camp, called "Ansar 4." He was questioned about his "wanted" brother's hiding place. Three interrogators beat him, he says, and the one name he remembers most is Assi. Perhaps Abu Assi, or Captain Assi. He was beaten particularly in his sex organs, his head was bashed against the wall, and he was strangled for alternating periods of time: fingers gripping both sides of his Adam's apple (demonstration), a look at the clock (demonstration), strangle and let go, strangle and let go. In one of the last interrogations he fainted and lost his voice. He was hospitalized after that. At present he still needs therapy for his posttraumatic stress disorder, as stated in his medical record. But psychotherapy is not a service publicly available in the Gaza Strip.

Qasem, twenty-four years old, was arrested at the end of last year and taken to an army base. He was seated there, shackled and blindfolded, and soldiers passing by cursed and kicked him time and again, for hours. From the base he was transferred to hospital and remained there for two days. He was not interrogated at all.

The two brothers at home—and needless to say, the brother held in administrative detention—have not been formally accused of anything nor brought to trial anywhere. All these arbitrary acts of harassment, against which the brothers cannot defend themselves and which are inflicted on them from the gray area of military activity or the twilight zone of the Shabak—call it what you will—are committed simply in order to make their lives so miserable that they finally betray their brother, whether they actually know of his whereabouts or not.

This story, Abu-Ashraf, I heard from them, from the family.

Is it true? If so, who gave you permission to treat an entire family this way because one of its older sons is "wanted"? To curse, beat, vandalize, arrest an elderly man and then release him somewhere in the middle of the night? And if the story is not true, and they themselves vandalized their own home, and learned the precise gestures of strangling and beating and shackling from their own violent society, as you might claim— then deny it loudly, or ask your superiors to deny it.

That family in the refugee camp. The youngster I saw a short while ago at Nasser Hospital in Khan Yunes, there after a week at the interrogation wing of the detention camp called "Ansar 2," who told me explicitly about being beaten to pulp and repeatedly locked inside a cell the size of a cupboard. Mahmoud Abu 'Araida from Al-Shaboura refugee camp, who has lodged a formal complaint against the Border police who arrested him on May 15 of this year and beat him inside their army vehicle and at the police station so brutally that when he was finally brought into custody at "Ansar 2" the doctor there required that he be hospitalized. Journalist Ari Shavit, who wrote about beatings and harassment and humiliations, and especially the moaning and sobbing and shouts that haunted him on his way to the shower and the dorms and the dining hall when he last served as a reservist at "Ansar 2," or as it is officially named, "Coastal Detention Facilities" (Haaretz, April 26, 1991). The B'Tselem (Israeli human rights organization) report "Interrogation of Palestinians during the Intifada: Harassment, 'Moderate Physical Pressure' or Torture?" published a few months ago, raising a moderate public outcry. (Now it seems that its many assertions of human rights violations, which cannot be characterized as merely exceptional occurrences, are being looked into via orderly procedures and are being addressed by the appropriate authorities and commissions, so the sensitive public at large need no longer be reminded of these testimonies and stories that continue to emerge from there and reach anyone willing to listen, and that are certainly known to the hundreds or perhaps thousands serving there in the military.) —If all of these, all of them, are lying, say so and prove it.

But if these testimonies are true, tell us—you, anonymous Abu Ashraf and Abu Rami and Captain Abu Nimer, acting under pseudonyms in Gaza, Rafah, Ramallah, Nablus, you, their superiors, our delegates—tell us: What rules and regulations are you obeying in order to guarantee our security? Do you actually believe this is the way to ensure our security, for months, years, generations perhaps?

This is the full version of my open letter to Abu Ashraf, some of which was published in *Haaretz* newspaper. I mailed it to three recipients, according to their appointed roles at the time:

the Committee on Shabak Interrogations; MK David Libai, chairman of the Knesset Committee for State Audit Affairs; and to the attorney general, Yosef Harish.

Following are the two responses I received.
   One:

> *I received your letter to me of June 30, 1991, and have requested that your complaint be looked into.*
>
> > *Respectfully yours, Prof. David Libai,*
> > *Chairman, Knesset Committee for State Audit Affairs*

Another:

> *I have received your letter, and having read it I remain deeply impressed by the harsh facts you recount. I shall do everything in my power to have its contents reach whoever is authorized to put things right.*
>
> > *Respectful greetings,*
> > *Yosef Harish*
> > *Attorney General*

I never heard from anyone again about the matter, and as far as I know, based on what the eye sees and the ear hears, none of the recipients have lifted a finger to "put things right."

# This Is Not My War!
## Summer 1991

You say these children don't play with marbles but throw stones and stones can kill, and that we have no choice but to respond violently to a violent war that is waged against us. I will not retort with the horrific statistics of how many of them have been killed by submachine guns and rifle fire and blows, versus how many of us have been killed by stones and knives. My answer is rather one of principle: There is no longer any justification for that statement made by all you good men among us; it is no longer an excuse for you, for us—who consider ourselves humanists, people with values. For this war that the Israeli army wages with truncheons and submachine guns against this army of children and youngsters, it is waged on the orders of a government whose official and declared policy is to stay here [the Occupied Territories] forever, not for reasons of security but out of deep ideological conviction, following its own logic with consistency. This ideology is not ours, my humanist compatriots of the beautiful, lofty values. We must not, you must not, allow any more children and youngsters, fathers, mothers, and human beings in general to be killed for it. Not in Jabalya in the Gaza Strip nor in Jerusalem's Baq'a neighborhood.

Go out and witness this filthy war for yourselves—you, many of whom have never set foot there. This is the war now waged daily in the alleys of refugee camps and cities, and this is the real war, not the despicable stabbings you are obsessed with, along with Shamir and Sharon and Geulah Cohen and "Gandhi" (Israeli politician Rehav'am Ze'evi)—members of our present democratic government—obsessed, as if content to find some kind of new excuse for inaction, content to feel a sense of horror and revulsion tinged with some satisfaction that here once more we have no choice but to sit quietly at home when the attackers have their say.

This war is not my war, nor is it yours—you humanists with values whom I address here—refuse to fight it: under such circumstances you must refuse!

# Nor Is This War Mine, Summer 2014

*Here I cede space to reports from two Israeli human rights organizations. Each one is acknowledged following the excerpt(s) from its report.*

On July 8, 2014, another round of hostilities broke out in Gaza. It was dubbed Operation Protective Edge. About fifty days later, the fighting ended in a ceasefire agreement between Israel and Hamas. During the fighting, which included an incursion by ground forces, the Israeli military launched strikes from air, sea, and land against thousands of targets. More than 2,200 Palestinians were killed, including hundreds of children. About 18,000 homes were destroyed or badly damaged, and more than 100,000 Palestinians were rendered homeless. Over the course of the fighting, Palestinians fired over 4,000 rockets and mortar shells from the Gaza Strip, mostly at civilian communities inside Israel. As a result of these rockets, five civilians were killed in Israel, including a four-year-old boy. Sixty-seven Israeli soldiers were killed in the fighting.

On the first day of the fighting, the military attacked the Kaware' family home. The house collapsed. Nine people, including five children aged seven to fourteen, were killed. This was just the first of dozens of air, sea, and ground strikes, which would become one of the appalling hallmarks of the fighting in Gaza this summer: bombings in which hundreds of people were killed—constituting more than a quarter of all of the Palestinians killed in the fighting. Time and again Palestinian families suffered grievous loss of life. In a single instant so many families were ruined, with the wreckage of their lives mirroring the devastation of their homes. . . .

At around 7:30 p.m. on July 20, 2014, the Israeli air force bombed the Abu Jame' apartment building in Bani Suheila near Khan Yunis. The three-story building had six apartments. One apartment was occupied by Fatmeh Abu Jame', age sixty-four, and one of her grandchildren. Fatmeh's five sons lived in the other five apartments Fatmeh's five sons lived in the other five apartments with their wives and children. A total of thirty-seven people lived in the building.

Twenty-four members of the family perished in the bombing: The mother Fatmeh, her son Yasser, four of her daughters-in-law, and eighteen of her grandchildren. Ahmad Sahmoud, a Hamas operative who is not a member of the family, was also killed. . . .

At around 1:30 a.m. on July 24, 2014, the air force attacked a house in Jabalya refugee camp in the northern Gaza Strip. One of the sons of the man who owned the targeted building is a member of Hamas's military branch. This may have been the reason for the attack. Testimonies collected by B'Tselem indicate that the military fired a warning missile, but local residents could not tell which home it was fired at and who was meant to leave. The house, which was vacant, was completely destroyed, and dozens of other nearby homes were damaged. One of them was the Abu 'Aytah home. . . . The hit to this home, which was partially destroyed, killed Mahmoud Abu 'Aytah's parents, two of his married brothers, and one of their sons.

*The people killed in the incident:*

The parents: Ibrahim Abdallah Ibrahim Abu 'Ayta, 66
            Jamileh Salim Eid Abu 'Ayta, 55
Their children: Mohammad Ibrahim Abdallah Abu 'Ayta, 32
            Ahmad Ibrahim Abdallah Abu 'Ayta, 31
            Ahmad's son: Adham Ahmad Ibrahim Abu 'Ayta, 4

. . .

On 2 August 2, 2014, around midday, the military attacked the home of the Abu Madi family in a-Nuseirat refugee camp, in the central Gaza Strip. The house collapsed on its occupants, killing six members of the family.

The three-story house was home to the extended Abu Madi family. Parents Yusef and Ra'isa Abu Madi lived with four of their children, aged ten to twenty-three, in an apartment on the second floor. Their four married sons and their respective families lived in the other apartments. In total, twenty-one people lived in the house.

*The people killed in the incident*

Yusef Da'ud 'Abd al-Mun'im Abu Madi, 68
            His sons: 'Abd al-Karim Yusef Da'ud Abu Madi, 23
            Hassan Yusef Da'ud Abu Madi, 17
        Amin Yusef Da'ud Abu Madi, 10

His grandchildren Yusef Shadi Yusef Abu Madi, 6
Hala Shadi Yusef Abu Madi, two weeks old

*B'Tselem report: "Black Flag: The Legal and Moral
Implications of the Policy of Attacking Residential
Buildings in the Gaza Strip," Summer 2014*

"I recall thinking that I couldn't give a damn about the Gazans right now, honestly. They deserve nothing. If they deserve something it's either to be badly wounded or die, that's what came to mind in those moments."

*Quoted in Breaking the Silence report:*
*"This Is How We Fought in Gaza, 2014"*

# EPILOGUE

The woman was at the beginning of her seventh life decade when she translated an anthology of stories and prose by Bertolt Brecht, and among them the following fable, about the man who learned to say no:

> One day, during the period of illegality, an agent entered the apartment of Mr. Eggers, a man who had learned to say no. The agent showed a document, which was made out in the name of those who ruled the city, and which stated that any apartment in which he set foot belonged to him; likewise, any food that he demanded belonged to him; likewise, any man whom he saw, had to serve him.
>
> The agent sat down in a chair, demanded food, washed, lay down in bed, and, before he fell asleep, asked, with his face to the wall: "Will you be my servant?"
>
> Mr. Eggers covered the agent with a blanket, drove away the flies, watched over his sleep, and, as he had done on this day, obeyed him for seven years. But whatever he did for him, one thing Mr. Eggers was very careful not to do: that was, to say a single word. Now, when the seven years had passed and the agent had grown fat from all the eating, sleep-

ing, and giving orders, he died. Then Mr. Eggers wrapped
him in the ruined blanket, dragged him out of the house,
washed the bed, whitewashed the walls, drew a deep breath
and replied: "No."

(translated by M. Chalmers)

Brecht had this fable told by a character he created in the beginning of his literary career, and it accompanied him throughout
thirty years of writing: Mr. Keuner, "he who thinks."

When the woman translated Brecht's stories about that Mr.
Keuner, five years had passed since she suddenly found herself
on her own, shaken and confused, wanting to get off the world.
But saying no was familiar to her from her earliest days. And
not due to her own rebellious nature and courage—she had
learned this from her parents. Especially from her mother, born
into an Orthodox Jewish family, who learned to say no from
the communists in the Warsaw Ghetto whom she befriended in
her youth. The mother had learned to do so even earlier, actually, for before she joined the communists and their forbidden
activities in the 1920s, she had already defied her parents and
become secular, like most of her new friends, all of them ghetto
residents. And thus, young adventurous rebel that she was, she
dared turn her back on her homeland a few years later and left
on her own to tour other parts. She worked and studied a bit
here, a bit there, and eventually on an extended journey that
took her away from Europe—fortunately in time, and for good.
     She traveled and traveled and traveled. From Vienna she
went east and south, to Athens, Istanbul, Damascus, and Bei-
rut, all the way to Haifa. There, tired of wandering, she found

employment as a maid and stayed. It was 1933, and she was twenty-three years old. She stayed in Haifa by chance—that's what she told her daughter; she was a communist, not yet a Zionist. Then the communist dream shattered and in its place she held on to the Zionist dream, which then also shattered, so that only the humanist dream remained. And so her daughter, who is now in her eighth life decade, was born at the foot of Mount Carmel, between the mountain and the sea, and was conscious of her mother's dreams and especially how they had been shattered, and thus in early childhood the daughter too had learned to say no.

But all along, due to the circumstances into which she was born, the history of clinging to dreams and seeing them shattered, and from all that "no" she repeated, she also learned to say yes: Yes to freedom, to the personal freedom of crossing borders— just like her mother—and beyond. Not ideological borders but human ones, real and imagined—both! Yes to breaking and undermining and tearing down barriers, outside of her and in- side as well, scorning anxieties and prejudices, surrendering to curiosity rather than to fear. Crossing with her body and spirit and mind barriers of walls and fences, ignoring borders of stone and metal and laws and decrees, and challenging the borders of the soul: borders of subjugation and obedience, and especially of fear. And defeating them.

With this kind of freedom she also discovered a new kind of joie de vivre.

*

This is what she wrote here, in these chapters of her personal- literary-documentary biography, wrote once, then twice, this version, then that, now mixing them and writing again for the third time. This is the epilogue of the present chapter of her life, beginning with the time when she suddenly found herself on her own, shaken and confused and wanting to get off the world, and continuing with the "no"—and then with the "yes" as well.

Yes and yes and more yes. Yes to meetings and shared travel, permitted and forbidden, driving and walking, overtly and covertly. Yes to the Gaza beach and the Tel Aviv beach. Yes to the friendship with women she has seen with and without their head coverings, in their weaknesses and strength, with whom she laughed in the car as they metamorphosed from fear to curiosity, then fun. Yes to the boys and girls with whom she rolled and spun round in the sand dunes of Nitzanim, with Momo the dog chasing after them, yet another free and merry and amusing creature who squeezed into the car with them to serve as yet another decoy when they crossed the checkpoint like a family out on a Friday picnic, a grandmother and her grandchildren.

✳

The story of all those yeses that evolved from all those nos is not over yet. "For from a certain point on there is no more going back. It is to that point that one has to arrive," wrote Kafka in a brief fragment that she translated at that time in her life, and thought that perhaps she had reached that point. The point where—in her own context, not his—the greatest yes of all is saying yes to personal and civil disobedience. Because

> if the injustice is part of the necessary friction of the machine of government, let it go, let it go; perchance it will wear smooth—certainly the machine will wear out . . . but if it is of such a nature that it requires you to be the agent of

injustice to another, then, I say, break the law. Let your life
be a counter friction to stop the machine.

Those were Henry David Thoreau's words written in the nine-
teenth century, her great inspiration which she follows in her
own world.
    And don't say that the friction is necessary, inevitable. It
isn't. This is what she thinks, the woman, and this is her greatest
no. People might say she is biased. About that she has nothing
more to say here: she has already said all that she had to say.